The
Low Oxalate Kitchen
Cookbook

The
Low Oxalate Kitchen
Cookbook

88 Recipes To Help Simplify A Low Oxalate Diet

Vincent Cilento

This book does not replace the advice of a medical professional.
Consult your physician before making any changes to your diet or regular health plan.

Paperback ISBN: 9798722480194

First paperback edition March 2021.

Cover art by Rochelle Ramos and Zahra Alipoursohi

Vincent Cilento
Low Oxalate Kitchen, LLC
www.lowoxalatekitchen.com

Preface

If you purchased this book, I want to start by saying thank you for supporting Low Oxalate Kitchen. As you may or may not know, it is my goal to make following a low oxalate diet easier than it has been up until this point.

The internet tells me that this preface should tell you, the reader, how and why this book is being written. If you are following a low oxalate diet, you probably already know why I decided to put this together. There are few trustworthy sources of information out there when it comes to oxalates, and even fewer reliable collections of recipes. So, here I am, trying to create one.

The "how" of this book is a bit different than you might expect. Although I do cook, I do it only because I have to eat, and I do not have enough money (yet, fingers crossed!) to eat all of my meals out or have someone else cook for me. I am in and out of the kitchen as quickly as I can be, and approximately three of the things I have ever cooked have made it into an organized recipe and onto a piece of paper.

For that reason, I decided to connect with a variety of chefs, nutritionists, and others who are the opposite of me, and just enjoy being in the kitchen and/or creating recipes.

This book is a compilation of recipes created by this group of people, specifically for a low oxalate diet. I have gone through each recipe to make sure they are not high in oxalates, and I provide an estimated oxalate content per serving for each of them.

This recipe book is organized by contributor, with each of their recipes following a quick introduction about them and their work. This is a very interesting group of people from all different backgrounds, countries and experiences, so make sure to read through their bios and connect with them if you have any questions or want to see what else they are up to!

I hope this is the first of many of these books to come. If you have any suggestions for me or know anyone who might want to contribute to any in the future, feel free to reach out at any time. My email address is lowoxalatekitchen@gmail.com.

Happy Eating!

An Important Note from the Author

Please read this section!

Please note, I am not a doctor, and nothing here is intended to be used as medical advice. Please consult a qualified medical professional before starting and while implementing a low oxalate diet.

Some people like to try and stay under 50 milligrams (mg) of oxalate for the day, but this is very difficult to do. For most people with kidney stones, staying under 75 or 100 mg per day is sufficient, in combination with other dietary modifications. Please double check this with your MD, so they can make a recommendation for you and your specific case.

If you are a kidney stone former, please ask your doctor for a 24-hour urine collection, and if they do not order one, please find a new doctor that will. Lowering oxalate intake is only half of the game when it comes to preventing kidney stones. There are many other factors involved, and the 24-hour collection can give you much more insight into your particular situation. For more on this, check out my podcast episodes with renal dietitian Melanie Betz (some of her recipes are also featured here). You can find the Low Oxalate Kitchen Podcast wherever you usually listen to podcasts, or on my website at lowoxalatekitchen.com.

This is not a book of low oxalate ingredients; it is a book of low oxalate recipes. Some of them contain medium oxalate ingredients. Each meal contains an estimated oxalate content for your convenience, but these are estimates. If you feel uncomfortable using a certain ingredient, feel free to leave it out or substitute it for something else I recommend or something that you would prefer.

Look for the Estimated Oxalate Content (EOC) in a green box like this on each recipe page. It will indicate how many mg of oxalate is in one serving of the meal.

EOC
~2mg

Introduction

As you probably already know, there is a bunch of confusion when it comes to the oxalate content of foods. The reasons for these discrepancies can be attributed to improvements in testing methodology, portion sizes, cooking methods, different types of the same foods, the maturity of foods and generic wording like "leafy greens" on different oxalate lists, among other things.

If you have not already, you can find more information on why this is by listening to the Low Oxalate Kitchen Podcast or joining my Mastering A Low Oxalate Diet Course that is available at lowoxalatekitchen.com/mastering-a-low-oxalate-diet-course.

For the most accurate and up-to-date oxalate list, I recommend the one provided by the Trying Low Oxalates group on Facebook. At the time of this writing, you have to join their group on Facebook, and follow the directions there to get access to their spreadsheet. I would share it with you here, but the document contains proprietary information, and is also way too comprehensive to fit into the pages of this book. In fact, any oxalate list that fits neatly onto one or two pages is most likely not as thorough as you will need it to be if you are really trying to reduce your oxalate intake. Do yourself a huge favor and get the list, and if you have trouble finding it or reading through it, let me know and I can help.

If that list is too overwhelming for you, the list from Harvard is probably the only other one that I would recommend. It does not do as good of a job as the Trying Low Oxalates list, but it is sufficient if the TLO list is too much.

The oxalate values in this book are current at the time of publishing in 2021. They are subject to change, which is a good thing, because it means testing methods are being improved and oxalate values are being updated. If you find any issues regarding this, please send me a nice email with your suggestion and I will take it into account for newer versions of this book, and for recipe books in the future.

Ingredients

As you know, getting everyone to agree on all of the same ingredients for a low oxalate diet is borderline impossible, so the following is a list of ingredients that are sometimes debated or confusing, but are included in this book, with some notes on each and/or the reasoning behind their inclusion.

I put this list together not to tell you what to eat or not eat, but so that I can share a little bit about what I have learned, so that you can make an informed decision about these and other foods you might choose to include in your diet.

- *Avocado* - Avocados are one of the foods that depends not only on the species, but also on the maturity level of it. Some foods will have lower oxalate contents as they get riper, and avocados are one of them. Very ripe, Hass avocados have been tested to be low oxalate. Other varieties have tested high, and Hass avocados that are not as ripe will be higher oxalate also.
- *Black Pepper* - Black pepper has gotten a bad rap as a high oxalate ingredient, because of the portion size that is generally tested. If you eat a tablespoon of black pepper, it will be high oxalate. If you eat a teaspoon, it will be medium oxalate. But, if you eat the same sprinkle that most people eat with a typical meal, you are unlikely to add a significant amount of oxalate. Black pepper has such a poor reputation that I decided to not even include it in the recipes, in case someone decides to skip this section and just starts sending angry emails. The recipes include white pepper as a lower oxalate substitute, but if you want to use very small amounts of black pepper, it will not add too much oxalate.
- *Blueberries* - Wild blueberries are the variety that have tested high, but the kind you usually see on the shelf in grocery stores in the US are low oxalate. If you do not want to use blueberries, that is up to you, and certainly fine with me.
- *Bone Broth* - Bone broth is itself low oxalate, but it has been suggested that the collagen in it can be converted into oxalates in the body. If this is a concern for you, you can use beef, chicken or vegetable broth in its place.
  - o *Bone broth* - cooked with bones, for a long time, has collagen
  - o *Stock* - cooked with bones, for a short period of time, has little collagen
  - o *Beef/chicken/vegetable broth* - cooked without bones, has even less or no collagen
- *Carrots* – Carrots are also generally excluded in low oxalate diets. However, carrots that have been boiled first, for about 10 minutes, move into the medium oxalate category, which is why small portions are included in some of the recipes here. The oxalate in foods is always in some ratio of soluble to insoluble, and some of the soluble oxalates are removed when they come in contact with hot water. Therefore, boiling or steaming vegetables with high ratios of soluble to

insoluble oxalate briefly before eating them can lower the oxalate content, provided that you discard the water afterwards.

- *Cinnamon* – Cinnamon is a very high oxalate food, so we use cinnamon extract in the recipes here in its place. You will find that some (but not all) extracts of high oxalate foods will be low in oxalate. When a high percentage of the oxalate in the food is insoluble, it will not dissolve into any water it is soaked or cooked in. The oxalates in the cinnamon sticks that are soaked to make cinnamon extract, are mostly insoluble, which is why the extract is low oxalate.

- *Ginger* - Fresh ginger is low in oxalates, but dried ginger powder is high. This happens with fresh vs. dried varieties of the same food sometimes because dried versions are basically concentrates. In a way, a teaspoon of dried ginger has much more ginger than a teaspoon of fresh ginger.

- *Hemp Seeds* - Usually labeled as high oxalate, but for larger quantities that most people will not eat. A teaspoon of hemp seeds or hemp hearts, which are hulled hemp seeds, has 2-3mg of oxalate.

- *Herbs de Provence* - Usually, you cannot generalize and say that any type of spice blend will be low oxalate. Italian, Mediterranean or other seasoning blends like a BBQ rub, curry powder, or something similar, can have such a wide variety of spices that the oxalate content of each would depend on the amount and ratio of spices in the blend. I have checked the ingredients list for over 10 different brands of Herbs de Provence, and they all seem to have pretty much the same spices. The ones that are in some and not in others are generally low or medium oxalate, except for one or two random ones that appear towards the end of the ingredients list, meaning that they are present in smaller quantities. For this reason, herbs de Provence can generally be considered low in oxalate, since it corresponds to a pretty standard blend of low oxalate spices. Morton & Bassett brand is the one I use since it has mostly low oxalate ingredients and only a couple of medium oxalate ones.

- *Kale* - Dino Kale, also called Lacinato or Tuscan kale, is low in oxalate. Red Russian kale is also low. Regular curly kale that is the most widely available in the United States can be high oxalate with larger portion sizes, but has more recently tested low also.

- *Lentils* – Brown, red and green lentils are the lowest. French green, white and black lentils are high oxalate. Pardina lentils, a smaller type of brown lentil, can also be high oxalate in larger quantities.

- *Onion Powder* - Onion powder has tested high before but has tested low since. In this situation, you can either err on the side of caution, or go with the most recent testing result since it is likely more accurate. You could also just take it easy on the portion size or use fresh onion if you would like.

- *Peppers* - Out of the different colors of bell peppers, red are the lowest oxalate. Green, orange and yellow are medium oxalate.

- *Potato Starch* - The overwhelming majority of potatoes are high in oxalate, so you will not see any in this recipe book. Potato starch, however, which is basically a dried potato extract, is low in oxalate, because the oxalates in potatoes are mostly insoluble and/or do not make it into the extract for one reason or another.

- *Pumpkin* - You will see pumpkin listed as low, medium and high. Fresh pumpkin is low. Canned pumpkin is in the medium range because water is taken out during the canning process, resulting in a more concentrated food, just like when drying spices. The high test results are for entire cans of it, meaning a larger serving size. Any food can be high oxalate if the serving size is large enough.

- *Rice Flour* – Rice flour's oxalate content will vary depending on the brand, because of the type of rice each is made from. This is a good time to have the TLO spreadsheet, because you can check for specific brands that have been tested, and stay away from the high oxalate ones.
- *Sesame Oil* - Oils in general are low oxalate foods, even if they are made from high oxalate foods. Oxalates are water soluble, but not fat soluble, so they do not make their way from the high oxalate food into the oil produced from it.
- *Soy Sauce* - Soybeans are high in oxalates, but soy sauce is not. Soybeans do not have a high enough percentage of soluble oxalate to result in a high oxalate soy sauce when the soybeans are soaked in water to make the sauce. Soy sauce is also eaten in such small quantities, that it is hard to get a significant amount of oxalate from it. If you are gluten free, you can substitute with tamari, and if you are watching your salt intake, you can substitute with coconut aminos.
- *Watercress* - Be careful when choosing foods like this, and others, that have similar names but are not exactly the same. Watercress is low in oxalate, but Chinese watercress is a completely different plant and is high in oxalate.

Table of Contents

Alexandra Cleanthous

Instagram: @thechoux_melbourne
alexandracleanthous.com

I was born in Cyprus, and cooking has always been a passion! After studying Political Science in Greece and France, I had that lightbulb moment where I knew I had to change careers, so I went and studied Culinary Arts at the Paul Bocuse Institute in Lyon, France. After working in Paris and Bordeaux, I moved to Melbourne, Australia where I worked in the catering industry. In March of 2020 I started "The Choux", a micro patisserie specializing in a delicious French dessert called "choux". To balance out the craziness of being a chef, I enjoy yoga, writing and the occasional Netflix marathons.

* Catch *Alex on Episode 4 of the Low Oxalate Kitchen Podcast!*

1

Black Eyed Pea Salad w/ Roasted Cauliflower & Pumpkin

Servings: 4 | Prep time: 15 min + soaking beans overnight | Cook time: 60 mins, or 30 mins for canned beans

INGREDIENTS

- 2 cups dried black eyed peas, soaked in water overnight, then drained [or 2 15-oz cans of black eyed peas, rinsed and drained]
- 4 cups cauliflower (around ½ a head), trimmed into large florets
- 4 cups pumpkin, peeled, cut into 1.5-inch cubes
- 1 yellow onion, diced
- Olive oil
- Fresh parsley for garnish

For the Vinaigrette

- ½ cup extra-virgin olive oil
- ¼ cup sherry vinegar (wine or apple cider vinegar also work!)
- 1 tsp seeded mustard

DIRECTIONS

1. Preheat oven to 350°F.
2. If cooking your own beans, place them in a large pot of water and bring to a boil over high heat.
3. Reduce heat to low and simmer for 45-60 minutes until tender.
4. Line a tray with parchment paper. Place the cauliflower and pumpkin into a bowl and drizzle with olive oil and season with salt. Use your hands to ensure the vegetables are well coated in the oil.
5. Spread onto the prepared tray and roast for 30-35 minutes or until tender and lightly golden, turning occasionally if needed. Set aside to cool.
6. In the meantime, prepare the vinaigrette. Pour oil into a mason jar. Add vinegar, mustard and salt. Cover and shake to blend.
7. Drain beans and add to bowl with roasted vegetables, diced onion. Coat with vinaigrette and serve.

EOC
~7mg

Coconut & Tamarind Prawn Curry

Servings: 4
Prep time: 15 min
Cook time: 15 minutes

EOC
~9mg

INGREDIENTS

- 1 13.5 oz can of coconut cream
- 3 Tbsp tamarind paste
- 2 garlic gloves, finely chopped
- 1 pound peeled, raw prawns
- 4 pieces of bok choy, washed and roughly chopped
- 4 spring onions finely sliced (keep the green and white part separated)
- 1 bunch of cilantro, chopped

DIRECTIONS

1. Heat a glug of oil in a large pot.
2. Fry the white part of spring onions until soft.
3. Add the garlic glove and stir for a couple of seconds. Be careful not to burn it.
4. Add the tamarind paste and coconut milk. Lower the heat and bring to a gentle simmer.
5. Let reduce for 5 minutes. Adjust the flavor if you would like more tamarind.
6. Add the prawn and bok choy then gently cook for 4-5 minutes.
7. Add salt and stir in half the cilantro.
8. Serve with steamed, white rice and garnish with the rest of the cilantro along with the green part of the spring onion.

Fried Cod with Tarragon Mayo & Cucumber Salsa

Servings: 4 | Prep time: 45 mins | Cook time: 15 mins

INGREDIENTS

Fish
- 8 small filets (about 1.5 pounds) cod, flounder, or any other white fish
- 6 Tbsp potato starch (maybe some extra if needed)
- Vegetable oil for frying
- 1 Tbsp butter

Tarragon Mayo
- 2 egg yolks
- ½ Tbsp mustard
- ½ Tbsp white wine vinegar
- 1 cup olive oil
- 1 Tbsp lemon juice
    OR
- 1 cup of good quality mayonnaise
    +
- 2 Tbsp of chopped tarragon leaves

Cucumber Salsa
- ½ of a medium sized cucumber
- 1 small red pepper
- 1 radish, or 2 if they are small
- Half a bunch of dill
- Half of a red onion
- Splash of olive oil and a squeeze of lemon juice

DIRECTIONS

Fish
1. Coat the fish in potato starch.
2. Heat up a non-stick frying pan to medium-high heat, pour in the oil and butter.
3. Place the fish pieces into the pan and fry for 3 minutes on each side or until golden brown.
4. Once both sides are brown and crisp, remove from the heat. Sprinkle some salt flakes if you have them or just some normal salt.
5. Serve the hot fish with the salsa and the mayonnaise on the side for the dipping.

Tarragon Mayo
1. If you are making your own mayonnaise, place 2 egg yolks in a bowl with mustard and white wine vinegar.
2. Whisk together and slowly add olive oil to emulsify. Add lemon juice, sea salt.
3. Seasoned with salt and stir in chopped tarragon to finish.
    OR
4. Mix chopped tarragon with a good quality mayonnaise of your choice.
5. Store in the fridge.

Cucumber Salsa
1. Dice all the vegetables and put in a bowl.
2. Chop the dill and mix into the salsa.
3. Season with salt, lemon juice and olive oil.
4. Leave in the fridge.

EOC
~10mg

Honey Panna Cotta with Pickled Blueberries

Servings: 4
Prep time: 15 mins, plus chilling
Cook time: 15 mins

INGREDIENTS

Panna cotta

- 2 ½ cups cream
- 1 ¾ cups milk
- 3 Tbsp + 2 tsp good quality honey
- 1 Tbsp powdered gelatin

Pickled blueberries

- ¼ cup water
- ¼ cup sugar
- ¼ cup vinegar of your choice (white wine, cider, champagne)
- 2 cups fresh blueberries

EOC
~8mg

DIRECTIONS

Panna cotta

1. Place 3 teaspoons of cold water in a small bowl and sprinkle with gelatin while mixing with a spoon. Set aside for 5 minutes or until spongy.
2. In a pot, add the cream, milk and honey.
3. Once the mixture is hot, add the gelatin and whisk well.
4. Using a ladle, pour the panna cotta mixture into the ramequins or jars.
5. Let set in the fridge at least 6 hours or better yet, overnight.

Pickled blueberries

1. Heat water, sugar and vinegar until sugar is dissolved.
2. Let cool down for a bit and then add the blueberries or your fruit of choice.
3. Put in fridge for at least a day.

To serve: Place blueberries on top of panna cotta with some of the pickling liquid. Enjoy chilled!

Sweet Whipped Ricotta and Lychee Pot

Servings 4 | Prep time: 30 mins

INGREDIENTS

- 1 ¼ cup good quality ricotta
- ¼ cup caster sugar
- 1 tsp freshly squeezed lemon juice
- Lychees in syrup

DIRECTIONS

1. Put the ricotta in a colander lined with paper towel.
2. Lightly press some more paper towel on the top to soak up as much water, then set aside for 20 minutes.
3. Whisk together the drained ricotta, sugar, lemon juice in the bowl of a food processor for about 5 minutes until smooth.
4. Scrape down the side of the bowl once or twice during whisking to ensure the cream is evenly silken.
5. If it is too loose, put in a damp cheesecloth or a tea towel for a couple of hours to drain excess moisture.
6. Divide into 4 bowls and serve with a couple of lychees cut in half.

EOC
~2mg

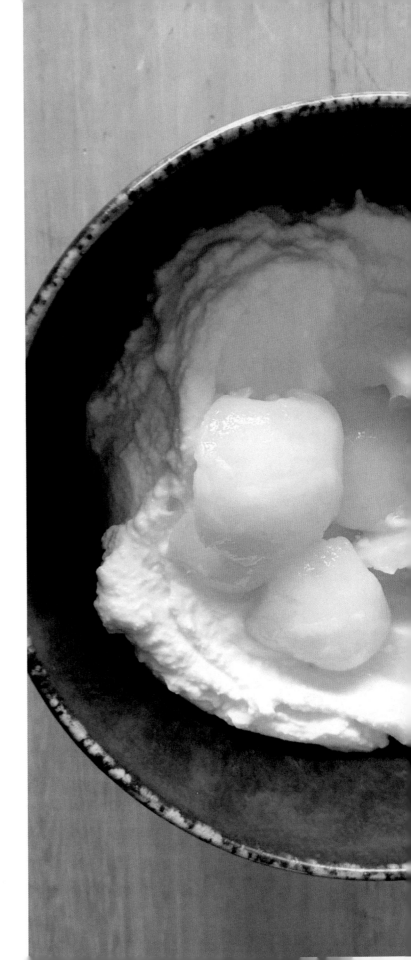

Alysha Melnyk

alyshathekitchenologist.com

Alysha is the Founder and Content Creator of The Kitchenologist©, a food blog dedicated to healthy eating and kitchen experiments. Alysha combined her background in biology with her passion for making food delicious, eye catching and accessible.

Local producers in Berks County, Pennsylvania inspire many of her recipes. She works with Taproot Farm during their summer Community Shared Agriculture (CSA) season, and has helped with recipe creation for a number of other local producers.

When she is not cooking in the kitchen or dreaming up a recipe, Alysha works full time as a Lead Educator at ECRI, an international medical nonprofit dedicated to improving patient safety worldwide.

She is also pursuing her Master's in Public Health at the Dornsife School of Public Health at Drexel University. Alysha finds her many career passions revolve around the power of knowledge, and that equipping people with the right tools and resources will help them make better informed decisions.

* Catch Alysha on Episode 2 of the Low Oxalate Kitchen Podcast!

Turnip Hash Browns

Servings: 1
Prep time: 10 mins
Cook time: 15 mins

EOC
~5mg

INGREDIENTS

- 2 turnips
- 1 large garlic clove
- 2 Tbsp olive oil

Optional for topping/serving: salt, fresh parsley and Greek yogurt/sour cream

DIRECTIONS

1. First, shred your turnips using a grater (I do not peel my turnips, but you can if you desire). Peel, then mince your garlic clove.
2. Press shredded turnip and minced garlic between paper towels or cloth towels. Repeat this a few times to try and remove as much extra moisture as possible.
3. Next, add the olive oil to your sauté pan and warm on medium heat for a few minutes.
4. Once oil is heated, add shredded turnip/minced garlic mixture into the oil and spread out in a thin layer.
5. Cook this layer for 5-10 minutes (it can vary from stove to stove, so keep an eye on the bottom for browning by gently lifting the edges with a spatula). If you feel the heat is too high, lower the heat.
6. Once bottom is browned, gently flip sections of the hash brown and allow to brown on the other side for around 5–10 minutes (once again, this depends on the heat of your stove top). Once hash browns are cooked, you may want to rest them on paper towels prior to serving to drain any residual oil.
7. Serve with Greek yogurt/sour cream and low oxalate herbs and spices like salt and parsley.

Rutabaga Fries
w/ Garlic Aioli

Servings: 2
Prep time: 15 mins
Cook time: 30 mins

EOC
~10mg

INGREDIENTS

- 1 large rutabaga
- 2 Tbsp olive oil
- 8 garlic cloves
- ⅓ cup mayonnaise (or mayonnaise alternative)

Optional for topping/serving: salt and fresh parsley

DIRECTIONS

1. Rinse your rutabaga, then cut into roughly uniform sized "fries" (aim for a similar thickness - about ½ inch thick for even cooking).
2. Peel your garlic cloves.
3. Preheat your oven to 420°F. Line a sheet pan with parchment paper.
4. While the oven is preheating, spread rutabaga fries and garlic cloves on the parchment lined sheet pan.
5. Toss rutabaga fries and garlic with 2 tablespoons of olive oil. Use your hands to make sure the rutabaga fries and garlic are evenly coated in the oil.
6. Arrange rutabaga fries and garlic on the sheet pan (preventing any overlap when possible).
7. Cook 15-20 minutes. You will notice light browning on the bottom of the rutabaga fries and garlic.
8. Gently flip fries and garlic, then cook for an additional 10-15 minutes (I cooked mine 10 minutes).
9. Remove the garlic cloves first, roughly mash them with a fork to desired consistency, and then combine with mayonnaise to create the aioli.
10. Serve garlic aioli with rutabaga fries. Sprinkle everything with low oxalate herbs and spices like salt and parsley.

Lacinato Kale Chips

Servings: 4
Prep time: 10 mins
Cook time: 6-7 mins

INGREDIENTS

- 1 bunch Lacinato kale
- 4 Tbsp olive oil

Optional for topping/serving:
salt and red chili flakes

DIRECTIONS

1. Preheat your oven to 425°F.
2. Rinse and destem your Lacinato kale.
3. Tear the leaves into bite sized "chip" pieces and pat dry with a paper or cloth towel.
4. In a large mixing bowl, combine kale pieces and olive oil.
5. Use your hands to massage the olive oil into the kale pieces so each piece is thoroughly coated (helping the chips crisp during baking).
6. Spread the kale pieces over two unlined sheet pans, making sure they do not overlap to allow for even cooking.
7. Cook kale chips for approximately 6 to 7 minutes until they are crisp but not burnt.
8. Allow kale chips to cool at room temperature (I recommend transferring them to a drying rack to cool so they do not soak in any residual oil).
9. Sprinkle with low oxalate herbs and spices like salt and red chili flakes.

EOC
~5mg

Quick Pickled Turnip, Apple and Cabbage Slaw

Servings: 4
Prep Time: 10 mins

Time in Refrigerator: Enjoy in a few hours, or leave overnight for a stronger pickling flavor

INGREDIENTS

- ½ cup turnip, diced
- ½ cup apple, diced
- ½ cup cabbage, diced
- ½ cup white vinegar or apple cider vinegar
- water

DIRECTIONS

1. First, clean a 16-ounce mason jar.
2. Dice your turnip, apple and cabbage into small pieces.
3. Add these to the jar and lightly press if needed to make sure all contents are below the base of the lid.
4. Add ½ cup vinegar into the jar. Fill the remaining space to the base of the lid with water.
5. Seal tightly and lightly toss the ingredients back and forth.
6. Place this in your refrigerator and enjoy in as soon as a few hours. For a stronger pickling flavor, wait overnight.

Just a reminder that this is a perishable food created through quick pickling methods, so please enjoy within 3 to 4 days.

EOC
~2mg

Portabella Mushroom and Arugula Sauté

Servings: 4
Prep time: 5 mins
Cook time: 20 mins

INGREDIENTS

- 6 cups arugula
- 2 cups portabella mushroom pieces
- 1 large garlic clove
- 2 Tbsp olive oil

Optional for topping/serving: salt and red chili flakes

DIRECTIONS

1. Add your oil to a sauté pan and warm on medium heat for a few minutes.
2. Next, add in portabella mushroom pieces and sauté around 5 minutes until tender.
3. After that, add in your minced garlic and cook for an additional 7 to 10 minutes until garlic and mushrooms are lightly browned.
4. Add in half of the arugula, cook for a few minutes until wilted, and then add second half of the arugula. Mix and toss this occasionally while cooking for an additional 5 to 7 minutes until most residual liquid cooks off.
5. Mix in low oxalate herbs and spices like chili flakes, salt and other seasonings as desired and serve.

EOC ~7mg

13

Anandita Sathyanarayana

YouTube: Visalam's Family Kitchen

My name is Anandita Sathyanarayana, and I am currently a student at Johnson and Wales University, majoring in Culinary Arts and Food Service Management. I am very fortunate to have grown up in the San Francisco Bay Area, a community that prides itself on eclectic cuisines, so at a very young age I began exploring cuisines outside of the South Indian food I was used to eating at home.

At this stage of my culinary journey, I have been able to hone my technical skills over the past few years, exploring various flavor profiles to generate my own recipes with whole ingredients. Combining my love for art and cooking, I am excited to showcase some of the recipes that have defined my journey. In the future, I strive to integrate my cooking with social media to display some of my work on a broader scale.

Blueberry Banana Muffins

Yield: 12 Muffins

Serving size: 1 muffin
Prep time: 15 mins
Cook time: 35-45 mins

INGREDIENTS

- 4 overripe bananas
- 4 eggs
- 3 Tbsp maple syrup or honey
- 1 Tbsp vanilla extract
- ⅔ cup coconut flour
- 1½ tsp baking powder
- ½ tsp baking soda
- ½ tsp salt
- ¾ cup blueberries (fresh or frozen)

DIRECTIONS

1. Preheat oven to 350°F.
2. Line muffin tin with paper muffin cups or non-stick cooking spray.
3. In a medium bowl, mash the overripe bananas. The riper the bananas are, the sweeter the muffins will come out.
4. Lightly beat the eggs before adding to the mashed bananas. Using a whisk, beat this mixture for a few minutes to ensure that the muffins come out light and fluffy.
5. Mix in the maple syrup/honey and vanilla extract to the banana mixture.
6. In a separate medium sized bowl, sift together the coconut flour, baking powder, baking soda, and salt.
7. Reserve 2 Tbsp of the flour mixture in a separate bowl.
8. Mix the remaining flour mixture into the banana mixture.
9. Coat the blueberries in the reserved 2 Tbsp of the flour mixture. This will ensure that the blueberries will not sink to the bottom of the muffins.
10. Fold the coated blueberries into the batter using a rubber spatula.
11. Using an ice cream scoop or ladle, spoon the batter into the muffin tins, making sure to get an even amount in each muffin tin cup.
12. Bake for 35-45 minutes, or until a fork inserted comes out clean and the tops of the muffins are golden brown.
13. Let cool for 5-10 minutes before removing from muffin tin.

EOC
~4mg

Garbanzo Bean Curry

Servings: 3 | Prep time: 30 mins | Cook time: 30-40 mins

EOC
~22mg

INGREDIENTS

- 2 15-oz cans garbanzo beans
- 2 Tbsp vegetable oil
- 1 white onion, diced
- 2 bay leaves
- 3-4 crushed cardamom pods
- 2 serrano peppers, cut lengthwise across middle
- 1 Tbsp ginger garlic paste
- 1 tsp chili powder
- 1 tsp mango powder
- 1 Tbsp ketchup
- ½ Tbsp tamarind concentrate
- ¼ cup water, plus additional as needed
- 2 Tbsp cilantro
- Salt to taste

DIRECTIONS

1. In a large pot, add the 2 cans of garbanzo beans including the water from the can. Bring to a boil, then lower to a simmer (medium heat) for 20 minutes. This will help soften the beans for the curry.
2. While beans are cooking, heat oil to medium high in a large sauté pan. Add bay leaves and chilis. Sauté for 2-3 minutes until fragrant.
3. Lower the heat to medium before adding ginger garlic paste, and quickly sauté until aromatic. Add diced onion once the ginger garlic paste is aromatic. Work quickly so the garlic does not start to burn.
4. Sauté this mixture until onions begin to turn translucent.
5. Add chili powder and mango powder. Stir the powders in and cook until onions are very soft and fragrant.
6. While this mixture is cooking, mix the tamarind concentrate with the ¼ cup water to dilute it slightly.
7. Add the tamarind mixture and ketchup to the onion mixture. Cook for several minutes until the oil from the pan begins to separate from the mixture, about 5-7 minutes. Add the cooked garbanzo beans, making sure to mash them slightly as you are mixing them in.
8. Add extra water if it's beginning to get dry and let cook for an additional 10 minutes to ensure all the flavors meld together.
9. Season with salt to taste, and stir in the cilantro, leaving a little to garnish.

16

Baked Cauliflower Wings

Servings: 5 | Prep time: 15 mins | Cook time: 35-40 mins

INGREDIENTS

- 1 head cauliflower
- 1 cup rice flour
- 1 cup water, plus more if needed
- Salt to taste

- 1 ½ tsp dried parsley
- 1 Tbsp garlic powder
- 1 Tbsp onion powder
- 2 tsp dried dill
- 1 tsp dried chives

- ¾ cup hot sauce (Frank's® RedHot® works well)
- 2 Tbsp butter

EOC
~10mg

DIRECTIONS

1. Preheat oven to 425°F.
2. Line a sheet pan with aluminum foil, and spray with nonstick cooking spray.
3. Cut cauliflower into evenly sized florets.
4. In a medium bowl, add rice flour. Gradually pour in water and stir until a batter forms. Add in dried herbs and stir.
5. Toss in cauliflower and make sure each floret is covered in seasoned batter.
6. Lay on prepared pan, making sure to separate the cauliflower out so they do not stick together.
7. Place in oven for 20 minutes.
8. Remove from oven and toss around. Place back in oven for an additional 5 minutes.
9. While cauliflower is cooking, melt the butter into the hot sauce.
10. Once cauliflower comes out, pour half of sauce onto cauliflower and toss. Place back in oven for 10 minutes.
11. After 10 minutes, toss the cauliflower in remaining sauce.
12. Serve with ranch or any preferred condiments.

Squash and Mushroom Taco with Rice Flour Tortilla

Servings: 3 (6 tacos total, 2 per serving) | Prep time: 45 mins | Cook time: 45 mins

INGREDIENTS

Tortilla

- 1 cup rice flour
- 1 cup water
- Salt to taste
- 3 Tbsp oil

Mango Salsa

- 1 mango, diced
- ¼ of a white or red onion, diced
- 1½ Tbsp honey
- 2 Tbsp cilantro, minced
- Juice of 1 lime/lemon
- ½ tsp chili powder
- Salt to taste

Guacamole

- 1 Hass avocado
- ¼ of a white or red onion, diced
- 2 Tbsp cilantro, minced
- Juice of 1 lime/lemon
- Salt to taste

Squash and Mushroom Filling

- 2 Tbsp avocado oil
- 2 yellow squash, diced
- 5-6 button mushrooms, minced
- 2 cloves garlic, minced
- ¼ of a white or red onion, minced
- Salt to taste

DIRECTIONS

EOC
~17mg

Tortilla

1. In a large bowl, drizzle water slowly into flour until it forms into a crumbly mixture. Cover and let sit for 10 minutes to let flour slowly absorb water.
2. After 10 minutes, add 2 Tbsp of oil to mixture, and knead until it forms into a bouncy dough.
3. Grease hands with remaining Tbsp oil, and split dough into 6 even balls
4. Roll each ball between 2 pieces of parchment paper into ⅛-inch tortilla.
5. Heat skillet to high heat and cook each tortilla for about 1-2 minutes per side, until small brown dots start forming.
6. Let the cooked tortillas rest on a plate under a kitchen towel.

Mango Salsa

1. Mix all ingredients together, taste for seasoning.
2. Cover and let sit in fridge to let flavors infuse with one another.

Guacamole

1. Mash avocado in bowl, add diced onion and cilantro.
2. Season with lemon/lime juice and salt to taste.

Squash and Mushroom Filling

1. Preheat oven to 400°F.
2. Toss the chopped squash with oil and salt.
3. Place on a greased sheet tray, making sure there is not too much overlap.
4. Place in oven for 20-25 minutes, stirring once after 10 minutes.
5. In a skillet, heat oil before adding onion.
6. Let onion cook until it is translucent before adding the minced garlic and mushroom.
7. Cook for 10-15 minutes, allowing the mushrooms to deeply caramelize.
8. By the time the mushrooms are done, the squash should also be ready as well.
9. Mix the two together if desired or serve separately.

Akki Roti (Rice Flour Vegetable Pancake) with Coconut Chutney

Servings: 6 (12 rotis total, 2 per serving)
Prep time: 30 mins
Cook time: 10 mins

INGREDIENTS

Roti

- 3 cups rice flour
- 2 tsp avocado oil, plus more in a small bowl
- 1 bell pepper, diced (any color)
- 1 cup carrot, boiled and mashed
- 1 zucchini, grated
- 1 cucumber, grated
- 1 red onion, diced
- 1 bunch dill, minced
- 1 bunch cilantro, minced
- 1 bunch fenugreek leaves, minced
- 1 cup water
- salt to taste

Chutney

- 2 tsp avocado oil
- ½ tsp asafetida
- 1 tsp chana dal (split chickpeas)
- 1 cup loosely packed shredded coconut
- 1 Tbsp grated ginger or ginger paste
- 1 tsp tamarind concentrate
- 2 Tbsp roasted chana dal (roasted split chickpeas)
- 2 serrano peppers
- ½-1 cup water

EOC ~18mg

DIRECTIONS

Roti

1. Mix all the ingredients except the flour, water, oil and salt.
2. After thoroughly mixed, add the flour slowly to coat the vegetables and herbs evenly.
3. Slowly drizzle in the water and mix until a firm dough forms. All the water measured might not be necessary.
4. Season to taste with salt.
5. Heat a cast iron skillet on high with 2 tsp of the avocado oil.
6. While the oil is heating, form the dough into small balls, placing each ball between 2 pieces of greased parchment paper and rolling to ⅛ inch thick. The rotis should be very thin to ensure a crispy exterior.
7. Once the oil is very hot and shimmering, remove the top piece of parchment paper and turn the roti out onto the cast iron skillet.
8. The roti will begin cooking and will slightly change color, indicating that the other piece of parchment can be peeled off.
9. Flip every few minutes, until desired crispness is acquired.

Chutney

1. Add the coconut, ginger paste, tamarind concentrate, roasted chana dal, and serrano peppers to a blender.
2. Drizzle in the water slowly while pulsing the blender until a paste forms. Set aside.
3. Heat 2 tsp avocado oil in a small skillet.
4. On medium heat, add in asafetida and chana dal, stirring until fragrant golden in color.
5. Add the hot oil mixture to the coconut mixture and stir.
6. Season to taste.

Ariana Chiarenza

Twitter: @ArianaChiarenza
achiarenzawriting.wordpress.com

Ariana Chiarenza is a writer and photographer with a degree in English Writing from Westfield State University. Her writing has been published in Persona Magazine, while her photography was featured in River River Journal and by Livers Bronze Railing Systems.

Coming from a family of Italian immigrants, food has been her passion since before she could talk. She takes great pride in her culinary culture and is honored to be able to share it through her writing.

Chickpea Pasta with Chicken and Summer Vegetables

Servings: 4 | Prep time: 15 mins | Cook time: 30 mins

INGREDIENTS

- ½ pound Banza chickpea spaghetti
- 1 zucchini, chopped into 1-inch cubes
- 1 yellow squash, chopped into 1-inch cubes
- 2-2.5 pounds of chicken breast, chopped into 1-inch cubes
- 1 yellow onion, diced
- 1 clove garlic, minced
- ½ cup low sodium chicken broth
- ½ tsp basil flakes
- Salt and white pepper to taste

DIRECTIONS

1. In a medium saucepan, heat 2 Tbsp oil of your choice. Brown chicken until cooked, searing for 2-3 mins on each side, then remove from pan.
2. In a separate pot, boil pasta as directed on box. Strain and rinse pasta with warm water.
3. In the same saucepan, add another Tbsp of oil and sauté onions for 3 minutes.
4. Add in garlic, zucchini, and squash. Stir, adding in salt, pepper, and basil flakes. Put the chicken back in the pan and add in chicken broth.
5. Cook on low heat for 5 minutes, then add in cooked pasta. Stir and serve.

EOC
~6mg

Apple Balsamic Salad

Servings: 4 | Prep time: 10 mins

INGREDIENTS

Salad
- 1 bag romaine lettuce
- ½ bag baby arugula
- 1 cup grated asiago cheese
- ¼-⅓ cup pumpkin seeds
- 1 Fuji apple, sliced

Dressing
- ½ cup balsamic vinegar
- ½ cup olive oil
- 3 Tbsp honey
- ¼ tsp thyme
- Salt and white pepper to taste

DIRECTIONS

1. Combine all dressing ingredients and stir thoroughly until well blended.
2. Combine arugula and romaine lettuce in a large bowl. Sprinkle in pumpkin seeds and cheese. Thinly slice the apple and add, stir to incorporate.
3. Add dressing to liking and serve.

Vanilla Mochi

Servings: 4 (8 total, 2 per serving) | Prep time: 20 mins | Cook time: 30 mins | Time in freezer: 3 hours

INGREDIENTS

- 1 cup rice flour
- 1 cup water
- ¼ cup white sugar
- ½ pint vanilla ice cream
- ½ cup corn starch
- ½ cup confectioners' sugar
- Plastic wrap

EOC
~6mg

DIRECTIONS

1. Scoop ice cream into 8 individual plastic wrap pieces, forming 3-inch balls. Wrap tightly and freeze.
2. Combine rice flour, sugar, and water into a microwave safe bowl. Cover with plastic wrap and microwave for 3 mins and 30 seconds. Take out and stir, then heat for an additional 15 to 30 seconds. Uncover and let cool to room temperature.
3. Combine cornstarch and confectioners' sugar in a plate. Roll rice dough into 3-inch balls and flatten into powder mixture.
4. Take ice cream out of the fridge and unwrap, then place the ice cream balls into the flattened rice dough. Wrap ice cream with dough, then wrap tightly in plastic wrap. Place all wrapped mochi in the freezer for at least 3 hours, then serve.

Slow Cooker Butternut Squash Soup

Servings: 4 | Prep time: 10 mins | Cook time: 6 hours

INGREDIENTS

- 1 butternut squash, peeled and chopped into 2-inch cubes
- 1 yellow onion
- 32 ounces chicken broth
- ¾ cup heavy cream
- ¼ tsp ginger, grated
- 2 tsp garlic powder
- Salt and white pepper to taste

DIRECTIONS

1. Peel and chop butternut squash into 2-inch cubes. Dice yellow onion and combine in a slow cooker. Add in chicken broth and seasonings and cook on low for 6 hours.
2. Remove squash and onions with a slotted spoon and blend in a food processor or blender until creamy, adding broth as needed for desired consistency.
3. Combine blended vegetables with half of leftover broth and heavy cream.

EOC
~10mg

Veggie Fried Rice

Servings: 4 | Prep time: 15 mins | Cook time: 30 mins

EOC
~8mg

INGREDIENTS

- 1 cup white rice
- ⅓ cup vegetable oil
- 1 ½ cup shredded green cabbage
- ½ yellow onion, diced
- 1 red bell pepper, diced
- ¼ tsp fresh ginger, grated
- 2 cloves garlic, grated
- 2-3 eggs, scrambled
- ½ tsp red pepper flakes
- Salt and white pepper to taste

DIRECTIONS

1. Prepare white rice according to package.
2. In a saucepan, heat oil. Add in onion until translucent, then add garlic and ginger. Add red bell pepper and cook until soft. Then add in cabbage. Push vegetables aside and cook eggs until scrambled, mixing with the vegetables when cooked.
3. Add in cooked rice, salt, white pepper, and red pepper flakes and combine with vegetables. Cook for 5 mins on low heat and serve.

Ella Davar, RD, CDN

IG: @nutritionistella
nutritionistella.com

Ella is a bilingual Russian-American Registered Dietitian, integrative nutritionist, certified health coach, yogi, theta healer and speaker with a passion for helping driven women streamline their wellness routine and accomplish a healthy balance in life with self-care.

She specializes in integrative anti-aging nutrition and lifestyle interventions to help driven people of all backgrounds manage weight, stress, diet, and various health conditions.

Ella received her education in Nutrition Science from New York University, and Integrative Nutrition Certification from the Institute for Integrative Nutrition.

Her upcoming book, *Driven Women Wellness: Your guide to self-care*, offers a cohesive list of priorities, plan of action and hacks that help her clients reach their wellness goals while managing busy lifestyles in a healthy way.

Grain Free Crackers

Servings: 6 | Prep time: 15 mins + 2 hrs out at room temp | Cook time: 30 mins

INGREDIENTS

- 1 cup / 135g sunflower seeds
- 1 cup / 140g flax seeds
- 1 cup / 95 g pumpkin seeds
- 2 Tbsp hemp seeds
- 4 Tbsp psyllium seed husks (3 Tbsp if using psyllium husk powder)
- 1 tsp fine grain Himalayan salt
- 1 Tbsp maple syrup
- 3 Tbsp melted coconut oil or ghee
- ½ cup / 150ml water

DIRECTIONS

1. Combine all dry ingredients in a bowl, stirring well.
2. Whisk maple syrup, oil and water together in a measuring cup. Add this to the dry ingredients and mix very well until everything is completely soaked and dough becomes very thick (if the dough is too thick to stir, add one or two teaspoons of water until the dough is manageable). Let sit out on the counter for at least 2 hours.
3. Preheat the oven to 350°F / 175°C.
4. Roll dough between parchment paper sheets using rolling pin until ½ inch thick. Cut into desired shape.
5. Place crackers in the oven on the middle rack and bake for 15-20 minutes. Remove crackers from the oven and turn it over to bake for another 15 minutes. Crackers are done when they are dry and crispy.

Store crackers in a tightly sealed container for up to five days.
Serve with a salad, butternut squash soup or yogurt dip.

EOC
~16mg

Quick and Easy Butternut Squash Soup

Servings: 3
Prep time: 15 mins
Cook time: 20 mins

INGREDIENTS

- ½ butternut squash, peeled and cubed
- ½ onion
- 1 apple
- 1 carrot, peeled and sliced
- 1 cup bone broth
- ⅓ teaspoon of Himalayan salt

Optional:
- 1 Tbsp of plain Greek yogurt
- 1 Tbsp of olive oil

DIRECTIONS

1. Bring a pot of water to a boil. Place the carrots in the water, and the squash, onion and apple together in a steam basket over the water for 10 min.
2. Discard water from pot.
3. Heat another pot with bone broth and combine it with vegetables.
4. Blend using an immersion or a standard blender.

Optional: serve with a dollop of plain Greek yogurt and a drizzle of olive oil.

EOC
~9mg

Green Goddess Morning Smoothie

Servings: 2
Prep time: 5 mins

INGREDIENTS

- ½ apple
- 1 small cucumber
- ½ banana
- 1 handful of lacinato kale
- A small handful of cilantro (optional)
- 1 date
- 1 tsp pumpkin seeds
- 1 tsp flax seeds
- 1 tsp of sunflower butter
- 1 scoop of protein powder of choice (whey, rice or pumpkin seed)
- ½ lemon, juiced

DIRECTIONS

1. Using a high-speed blender, mix all of the ingredients together.
2. Serve and sip!

Optional topping: coconut flakes!

EOC
~10mg

Coconut Flour Pancakes

Servings: 2
Prep time: 10 mins
Cook time: 10 mins

INGREDIENTS

- ¼ cup coconut flour
- 3 large eggs
- 2 Tbsp coconut oil
- 2 Tbsp maple syrup
- 1 tsp baking powder
- 1 tsp vanilla extract
- ⅛ teaspoon fine sea salt

DIRECTIONS

1. In a large bowl, combine the coconut flour, eggs, oil, maple syrup, baking powder, vanilla extract, and salt. Use a whisk to stir it all together, breaking up any clumps.
2. In a greased skillet over medium-low heat, add 3 tablespoons of the pancake batter and allow it to cook until bubbles start to form in the middle of the pancake, about 3-4 minutes. Flip the pancake and let it cook on the other side, about 3 more minutes, or until both sides are golden. Do not be tempted to increase the heat to speed up the cooking time, or the outsides of the pancake might burn before the inside is cooked through and fluffy.
3. Repeat with the remaining batter, making roughly 6 small pancakes. Serve warm with your favorite toppings like fruit compote or plain probiotic yogurt. Leftover pancakes can be stored in an airtight container in the fridge for up to 3 days.

EOC
~2mg

Herb Lemon Chicken
with Sauteed Bok Choy and Jasmine Rice

Servings: 2 | Prep time: 15 mins | Cook time: 60 mins

EOC
~13mg

INGREDIENTS

Chicken

- 2 chicken thighs
- 1 tsp of herbs de Provence
- 1 lemon
- ½ cup of water
- Salt to taste

Rice

- 1 cup of jasmine white rice
- 2 cups of water
- 1 tsp of coconut oil
- a pinch of Himalayan salt

Sauteed Bok Choy

- 1 pound baby bok choy
- 1 ½ Tbsp coconut oil or extra-virgin olive oil
- 3 garlic cloves, minced
- Pinch of crushed red pepper flakes
- Himalayan salt
- ½ lemon, in wedges

DIRECTIONS

Chicken

1. Preheat the oven to 375°F.
2. Drizzle olive oil in the bottom of Dutch oven.
3. Rinse chicken in cold water. Pat dry.
4. Sprinkle salt and herbs de Provence on both sides of the chicken.
5. Place chicken thighs in Dutch oven, add water.
6. Add lemon slices to the pot.
7. Cover and place inside oven. Cook for about 30-40 mins, or until internal temperature is 185°F.
8. Remove the lid and allow the chicken to brown for 5-10 minutes.
9. Let chicken rest before serving.

Rice

1. Combine rice with water in a small Dutch oven.
2. Add coconut oil and bring to a boil.
3. Place the lid on the Dutch oven and set the timer for 15 minutes.
4. Turn off the heat.
5. Remove from the burner it was cooked on to a cold burner.
6. Do not remove the lid or stir the rice.
7. Set timer for 15 minutes. When the timer goes off your rice will be ready.
8. Stir and fluff rice.

Sauteed Bok Choy

1. Place bok choy into colander and rinse with cool water, rubbing any grit or dirt from between leaves. Trim ends and slice bok choy in half lengthwise.
2. Add the oil, garlic and red pepper flakes to a wide room-temperature skillet.
3. Place over medium heat and cook, stirring occasionally, until the oil begins to bubble around the garlic, but before garlic starts to turn light brown.
4. Toss in the bok choy and spread into one layer. Sprinkle with about ¼ teaspoon of salt then cook, without stirring, until the bottom is starting to turn brown, about 2 minutes.
5. Flip then cook for another 2 minutes or until the green leaves have wilted and the white bottoms are beginning to soften, but still have some crunch.
6. Transfer to a platter then squeeze ½ of a lemon on top.

Ilene Kapelner, MA, RD, CDE, CDN

KumaShake.com
IG: @kumashake_inc

Ilene is a Registered Dietitian, Certified Dietitian-Nutritionist and Certified Diabetes Educator. She received her Master's in Nutrition from NYU. Ilene has 27 years of experience in the field of nutrition in various settings.

She currently has a private practice in nutrition, specializing in weight loss and diabetes, and is a provider for 1199, Aetna, Cigna, Empire, GHI and Oxford United Health Care, among others.

As a nutritionist in an ALS clinic at Beth Israel Mt. Sinai Hospital in New York City, she also helps patients with Lou Gehrig's disease improve their quality of life.

Ilene believes in a low carb/ketogenic diet and is interested in research that has shown that it may potentially be beneficial for conditions such as Epilepsy, ADHD, Autism, MS, Parkinson's, Crohn's, and Cancer.

Ilene's enthusiasm, caring nature, and excellent listening and counseling skills enable clients to feel comfortable working with her. She finds great satisfaction in helping people.

When Ilene isn't working, she enjoys traveling and being active outdoors hiking/walking. She also enjoys cooking and experimenting in the kitchen.

Together, with her daughter and son, they engineered the KUMA Shake, a ketogenic, dairy-free, gluten-free, on-the-go snack that has zero net carbs and is made with healthy fats. The new Kuma Shake is available on Amazon.

Oven Baked Mediterranean Flounder

Servings: 2
Prep time: 10 mins
Cook time: 30 mins

INGREDIENTS

- ½ pound flounder
- 4 Tbsp butter
- Juice of 1 lemon
- 1 Tbsp fresh parsley, chopped
- ¼ cup red pepper, chopped
- ¼ cup green pepper, chopped
- ¼ cup yellow onion, chopped
- 1 oz crumbled feta cheese
- 2 Tbsp capers
- Slices of lemon for garnish

DIRECTIONS

1. Place flounder on foil lined baking sheet, on top of 2 Tbsp of butter.
2. Top flounder with chopped peppers, onion, cheese, capers, lemon juice and 2 Tbsp butter.
3. Fold up corners of foil to cover everything and bake at 350°F for 30 minutes.
4. Garnish with slices of lemon and fresh parsley.

EOC
~9mg

Stuffed Cabbage

Servings: 2
Prep time: 20 mins
Cook time: 90 mins

INGREDIENTS

Sauce

- 2 Tbsp oil
- 1 Tbsp honey
- ¼ cup chopped onions
- ¼ cup chopped cabbage
- Juice of 2 lemons
- 1 can cranberry sauce
- 1 cup ketchup

Filling

- ½ pound ground beef
- 2 Tbsp rice
- 1 Tbsp potato starch
- Salt and white pepper to taste
- 1 egg

Additional

- 1 head of green cabbage

DIRECTIONS

1. Boil cabbage just enough to soften the leaves, to be able to remove them easily. Remove about 6-8 leaves and set aside.
2. In a separate bowl, mix all ingredients for the meat filling together. Form golf size balls and roll them into
   the cabbage leaves, tucking in the sides.
3. Add sauce ingredients to a pot and bring to a simmer for 10 minutes.
4. Place meat filled cabbage balls carefully into the pot. Cook on very low flame for 1 ½ hours.

EOC
~12mg

This dish tastes even better the next day!

No Bake Coconut Bites

Servings: 3 | Prep time: 15 mins

EOC
~10mg

INGREDIENTS

- 4 dates
- 2 Tbsp pumpkin seeds
- 2 Tbsp sunflower seeds
- 4 Tbsp sunflower butter
- 1 Tbsp coconut oil
- 2 Tbsp amaretto
- 1 Tbsp honey
- ¼ cup Rice Krispies
- Shredded coconut

DIRECTIONS

1. Place all ingredients into food processor, except Rice Krispies. Chop into small crumbs.
2. Transfer to bowl and mix in Rice Krispies.
3. Scoop out mixture with hands, and form golf size balls.
4. Roll each one into shredded coconut.
5. Store in refrigerator or freezer.

Rice Noodles with Sunflower Paste

Servings: 2
Prep time: 15 mins
Cook time: 15 mins

INGREDIENTS

- ½ pound rice noodles
- ½ cup sunflower butter
- ¼ cup hot water
- 1 tsp sugar
- ½ tsp cayenne pepper
- 2 Tbsp soy sauce
- 1 Tbsp apple cider vinegar
- 2 Tbsp sesame oil
- Red pepper
- Cucumber

DIRECTIONS

1. Boil rice noodles, rinse under cold water when done.
2. In a separate bowl, blend sunflower butter and hot water well, until smooth.
3. Add sugar, cayenne pepper, soy sauce, vinegar, oil and mix well.
4. Stir the noodles into sauce until evenly mixed.
5. Garnish with thin, bite size slices of cucumber and peppers.
6. Serve at room temperature or cold.

EOC ~23mg

Cauliflower Pizza

Servings: 2
Prep time: 20 mins
Cook time: 45 mins

INGREDIENTS

Crust

- 1 bag of frozen cauliflower rice
- 1¼ cup shredded mozzarella cheese
- ¼ cup grated parmesan cheese
- 1 egg
- ⅛ tsp flax seed
- Fresh basil for topping
- Crushed red pepper

Sauce

- ¼ cup ketchup
- ¼ tsp onion powder
- ¼ tsp garlic powder
- ¼ tsp thyme
- ¼ tsp rosemary
- ¼ tsp sugar
- 1 Tbsp water
- 1 Tbsp olive oil

DIRECTIONS

1. To make the crust, microwave the cauliflower rice for 5 minutes, open bag and let cool.
2. Place the cauliflower in a clean dish towel or cheese cloth. Squeeze, removing as much water as possible. Do not skip this step!
3. Mix the squeezed cauliflower in a bowl and with parmesan cheese, 1 cup of mozzarella, and egg.
4. Place parchment paper on a baking pan or pizza stone. Sprinkle paper with flax seeds.
5. Flatten the cauliflower mixture on top of the seeds to form a thin, round crust.
6. Bake at 450°F for 20 minutes until brown spots appear. Flip crust and continue baking for 15 minutes.
7. Sauté sauce ingredients for 10 minutes.
8. Take out of oven, top with sauce, remaining ¼ cup of mozzarella cheese and favorite toppings.
9. Return to oven, bake until cheese melts, about 10 minutes.
10. Take out of oven, add fresh basil, crushed red pepper and sprinkle of olive oil.

EOC
~8mg

39

Jessica Malone

liveandletlivenutrition.com
IG: @liveandletlive_nutrition

Jessica is a Certified Nutritionist living in San Diego, California. She has just recently graduated with a Master's Degree in Nutrition from Bastyr University California, where she obtained formal instruction in therapeutic nutrition and education.

She founded Live and Let Live Nutrition in 2018 to serve as a medium to spread her nutrition knowledge and share her most successful food creations. Although the brand was originally meant to be an homage to plant-based eating, her graduate studies have taught her that there are many ways to eat and live healthfully.

Live and Let Live Nutrition is now centered around the message that we can all choose to live (and eat) the way that best suits us as individuals, and we can live amongst others doing the same for themselves. It is about doing what works for you, whilst keeping an open mind to difference. If this means putting bacon on a veggie burger, or vegan cheese on your eggs, you are living the Let Live philosophy.

At the end of the day, Jessica hopes to teach others that a plant-forward lifestyle is the best and most supported way to achieve health and longevity, but that it never has to be the "all or nothing" approach that it is so frequently portrayed as.

Garlic and Rosemary Mashed Cauliflower

Servings: 2 | Prep time: 15 mins | Cook time: 20 mins

EOC
~10mg

INGREDIENTS

- 1 large head of cauliflower
- 1 Tbsp high heat cooking oil
- ½ cup (8 Tbsp) unsalted grass-fed, organic butter
- ¼ cup water (or vegetable stock)
- 1 large bulb of garlic
- 2 Tbsp of dried rosemary
- 2 tsp white pepper
- Salt, to taste

Optional garnish: 1 sprig of fresh rosemary

DIRECTIONS

1. Preheat your oven to 400°F.
2. Wash and chop the cauliflower into small, bite-sized pieces, including the stalk. Spread onto an aluminum lined baking tray. Toss with cooking oil.
3. Trim the head off the garlic bulb and place cut side down on the baking tray.
4. Bake the tray for 15-20 minutes, or until the cauliflower has softened and darkened, and the garlic is aromatic and slightly golden.
5. In a large saucepan, gradually melt the butter. Add in the roasted cauliflower, garlic cloves from the bulb (careful not to burn your fingers), rosemary, and white pepper. Cover with a lid to let steam for about 5 minutes.
6. Using a handheld immersion blender (or transfer to a high-powered blender), blend until smooth. Use the water (or vegetable stock) incrementally to help with blending, being careful not to add too much at a time and risk a runny mash.
7. Taste and season with salt, top with fresh rosemary and serve.

Note: This dish is good cold as a sandwich spread, or heats well in the microwave, covered.

Cheddar and Chive Biscuits

Servings: 8 (Yield: 8 biscuits) | Prep time: 15 mins | Cook time: 18 mins

EOC
~4mg

INGREDIENTS

- ½ cup roasted chickpea flour*
- ½ cup coconut flour
- 1 cup potato starch, more for kneading
- 3 Tbsp of cornstarch
- ½ Tbsp baking powder
- 1 tsp baking soda
- ½ tsp salt
- ½ tsp garlic powder

- ¼ tsp white pepper
- ⅔ cup cheddar cheese, shredded
- 2 Tbsp fresh chives, chopped (or 1½ Tbsp dried chives)
- 8 Tbsp grass fed, unsalted butter, chilled
- 1 cup milk of preference, chilled
- 1 tsp apple cider vinegar (or lemon juice)

You can dry toast regular chickpea flour for the same effect. Just stir the chickpea flour in a dry skillet over medium heat until the flour goldens in color.

INSTRUCTIONS

1. Preheat your oven to 375°F.
2. In a medium sized bowl, add the milk and vinegar and allow to curdle. Place back in the fridge.
3. In a large mixing bowl, add the dry ingredients and mix thoroughly. (Note: Sifting the flours, powders, and starches is a great idea here, but not necessary.)
4. Add in the cheese and rosemary, mix again.
5. Pull the premeasured butter out of the fridge and cut into the dry ingredients with either a pastry cutter, a fork, or your hands, until small pieces of butter are formed throughout.
6. Pull the chilled, curdled milk out of the fridge and add to the dry ingredients. Fold gently until the batter just comes together.
7. On a clean surface sprinkled with a bit of potato starch, turn your batter out of the bowl and form flat rectangle, a few inches

thick, with your hands. Fold the batter in half over itself. Repeat two times to create layers in the batter.
8. Flatten once more to a few inches thick and using a biscuit cutter, or the bottom of a tall glass, cut out your biscuits. Reform the batter and continue biscuit cutting until the batter is gone.
9. Place the biscuits an inch apart on a parchment or silicone lined baking sheet and pop in the oven for about 18 minutes, or until a slight golden-brown color is achieved.
10. Optionally, take the biscuits out of the oven in the last 3 minutes and coat with a little melted butter (or a beaten egg), and sprinkle with leftover rosemary. Place back in the oven.

Serve immediately or allow to cool before placing into a storage container.

Tuna (or Veggie) Sushi

EOC ~17mg
for 2 tuna rolls

EOC ~22mg
for 2 veggie rolls

Servings: 2 (makes 4 tuna or 4 veggie rolls)
Prep time: 20 mins | Cook time: 20-30 mins

INGREDIENTS

Rice
- 1 cup dried sushi rice
- 1 cup water
- 1 cup riced cauliflower*
- 2 Tbsp rice vinegar
- 1 Tbsp toasted sesame oil
- 1 tsp sugar
- 1 pack nori sheets

Tuna Roll
- 3 oz of extremely fresh, raw tuna (or smoked salmon)
- 1 small avocado, sliced
- 1-2 Tbsp preferred cream cheese
- 1 punnet of broccoli sprouts

Veggie roll
- 1 punnet of shiitake mushroom, sliced
- 1 Tbsp of high heat cooking oil
- 1 Tbsp of toasted sesame oil
- 1 Tbsp of coconut aminos
- 1 red bell pepper (or cucumber), julienned
- 1 small avocado, sliced
- 1-2 Tbsp of preferred cream cheese
- 1 punnet broccoli sprouts

Optional for serving
- Coconut aminos
- Sweet (or spicy) chili sauce
- Pickled ginger
- Wasabi paste

A head of cauliflower may be used and pulsed in a food processor, or blender, until small pellets are formed.

INSTRUCTIONS

1. In a fine strainer, rinse the rice in cold water until the water runs clear. (This step eliminates excess starch that will otherwise make your rice too mushy.)
2. In a rice cooker, or pressure cooker, cook the rice with the water. (Note: Rice cookers will have a pre-set setting, so follow your manufacturer's instructions. Using the pressure cooker, cook for approximately 5 minutes of pressurized cooking, followed by 10 minutes of depressurization (or natural depressurization). You can also cook the rice in a pot on the stove, covered, at medium low heat for approximately 15-20 minutes, or until the water is absorbed.)
3. To the same rice pot, add in the riced cauliflower, vinegar, sesame oil, and sugar. Stir to combine. Cover with a lid and allow the steam to soften the cauliflower.
4. If making vegetarian rolls, heat 1 Tbsp of cooking oil in a skillet over medium heat and sauté the sliced mushrooms for approximately 5 minutes, or until the mushrooms become soft and juicy. To aid with the juiciness, coat mushrooms with the sesame oil and coconut aminos. Set aside to cool.
5. While the rice mixture cools, prepare the remaining sushi ingredients for rolling (i.e. slice the tuna into thin strips, slice up the avocado or other ingredients) and prepare your sushi rolling station with a clean place to roll, nori sheets, bamboo sushi rolling mats*, plastic wrap, and a sharp knife.
6. To roll the sushi: Begin by placing a nori sheet smooth side down on a bamboo mat or square of plastic wrap. Cover the nori sheet with a thin layer of the rice mixture, leaving about ¼ inch bare at the top and the bottom edge of the nori. At the bottom third of the rice covered nori, lay your filling ingredients horizontally across the sheet, being diligent not to pack in too much of the ingredients. Next, roll the bottom of the nori sheet over your filling ingredients using the mat or plastic wrap as a form guide. Once the bottom edge of the nori sheet has made contact with the inside of the roll, give a gentle squeeze to the length of the roll. Then, pull back the bamboo mat or plastic wrap, and continue rolling in this manner

until the top edge of the roll is met. Once the whole roll is formed, give a final squeeze to ensure the roll is compact.

7. Using a sharp knife dipped in hot water, gently cut your sushi roll into sushi pieces of desired thickness. Between cuts, wipe the knife clean and dip in more hot water to ensure clean cuts.

8. Serve on a large platter with saucers of dipping sauce and optional accompaniments. Be diligent to eat the raw tuna rolls as soon as possible to avoid rancidity.

Bamboo sushi rolling mats are recommended for perfect sushi rolls, but plastic wrap and careful hands work just as well. Any leftover sushi ingredients can be repurposed into a quick fried rice or poké bowl the next day.

Zucchini Lasagna with Red Pepper Sauce

Servings: 6 | Prep time: 35 mins | Cook time: 20 mins

EOC
~23mg

INGREDIENTS

Red pepper sauce
- 4 red bell peppers, quartered
- ½ sweet onion, quartered
- 1 large bulb of garlic
- 1 Tbsp high heat cooking oil
- 1 tsp salt
- 1 tsp white pepper
- 1 tsp dried tarragon
- 1 Tbsp dried basil
- 1 Tbsp smoked paprika
- 1 tsp cayenne pepper
- 1-2 Tbsp balsamic vinegar

Bolognese filling
- 12 oz of grass fed, ground beef (or organic ground turkey, or 1 ½ cup cooked lentils if vegetarian)
- ½ sweet onion, diced
- 1-2 cloves of garlic, minced
- 1 punnet of cremini mushrooms, diced
- 1 Tbsp high heat cooking oil
- 1 Tbsp red pepper flakes

Ricotta filling
- 30 oz (2 15-oz tubs) organic ricotta cheese
- 1 Tbsp red pepper flakes
- 1 Tbsp dried basil leaves
- 1 tsp white pepper

In place of noodles:
- 2-3 zucchini, washed and trimmed

Topping
- ½ cup mozzarella or ¼ cup parmesan cheese

DIRECTIONS

1. Preheat your oven to 400°F.
2. Place the prepared bell pepper and onion on an aluminum foil lined baking tray. Toss with the cooking oil and salt. Trim the head of the garlic bulb to expose a few of the cloves and place cut side down on the baking tray. Bake for approximately 15-20 minutes, or until all contents have softened and developed color. Toss the peppers and onions halfway through.
3. In a blender (or food processor), pulse the baked peppers, onions, and roasted garlic cloves (once cool enough to handle) with remaining sauce ingredients until desired consistency is achieved. Set aside.
4. In a deep skillet (or shallow stock pot), heat the cooking oil and sauté the diced onion. Once translucent, add in the minced garlic, red pepper flakes, and ground beef. Allow to brown for 1-2 minutes, then add in the mushrooms and continue sautéing until all the beef is cooked through and the mushrooms have softened. (Note: If using cooked lentils instead of beef, sauté the mushrooms with the onions for 1-2 minutes before adding in the lentils and remaining ingredients.) No need to overcook the bolognese filling, as it will be baked once assembled. Once cooked, turn off the heat and stir in the red pepper sauce. Set aside.
5. In a medium size bowl, mix the ricotta ingredients. Taste and adjust seasoning to preference.
6. Using a mandolin, vegetable peeler, or sharp chef's knife, thinly slice the zucchini lengthwise to form zucchini lasagna "noodles". (Note: The thinner the zucchini noodle, the less baking time the finished lasagna will need.)

7. Layering the lasagna: In a medium-large baking dish, begin with a thin layer of bolognese sauce. Then, layer zucchini noodles across the bottom of the dish in one direction, partially overlapping each other. The remaining layers may be done to preference, but I recommend another layer of bolognese sauce directly over the zucchini noodles, followed by a thin spreading of the ricotta filling. Repeat layers until the dish is filled. (Note: In order to cut more easily, zucchini noodle layers should be laid in opposite direction from the one before (i.e. lay vertically if previous layer was horizontal).

8. Top the final layer of lasagna with mozzarella or parmesan cheese.

9. Place the lasagna in a 400°F oven for approximately 15 minutes. It will be done once the filling begins to bubble and the cheese topping has melted and browned.

10. Allow to cool and set for approximately 10 minutes before cutting and serving. Serve with additional sprinkling of red pepper flakes if more spice is desired.

Peaches and Cream Waffles

Servings: 3 | Prep time: 15 mins | Cook time: 10 mins

EOC
~5mg

INGREDIENTS

- 1 cup roasted chickpea flour*
- 4 Tbsp cornstarch
- 1 tsp baking powder
- ½ tsp baking soda
- 1½ Tbsp sugar

- 1½ tsp apple cider vinegar (or lemon juice)
- 1 tsp vanilla extract
- 1 tsp vegetable oil
- 1¼ cup milk of choice

- 1 cup of preferred yogurt (Greek recommended)
- 1 Tbsp maple syrup (or honey)

- ¼ tsp of cinnamon extract
- 1 peach, sliced
- Cooking oil spray

* You can dry toast regular chickpea flour for the same effect. Just stir the chickpea flour in a dry skillet over medium heat until the flour goldens in color.

DIRECTIONS

1. Set waffle maker to medium heat setting.
2. In a small mixing bowl, add the milk, vinegar, oil, and vanilla extract. Set aside to allow curdling.
3. In another small bowl, mix the yogurt, maple syrup, and cinnamon extract until thoroughly combined. Taste and adjust as desired. Set aside for assembly.
4. In a medium sized bowl, add the dry ingredients and mix thoroughly. (Note: Sifting flours, starches, and powders is a good idea, but not necessary.)
5. Add wet mixture into dry mixture and stir gently until combined. Batter may be a little clumpy.
6. If waffle maker instructions call for cooking oil, spray the iron, then add about ½ cup of batter, depending on the size of your iron. Close and let cook according to waffle maker instructions. (Note: Some irons may require doubled cooking times to allow the waffle to crisp up.)
7. To serve, top with a generous dollop of the sweetened and spiced yogurt, the sliced peaches, and a drizzle of maple syrup, if desired.

Kyle Baumgartner

Kyle has trained under chefs from the United States and Europe.

With a long career committed to excellence in the hospitality industry, his personal ethos includes using ingredients found locally and in the current season, with an affinity for low waste.

He has assisted directly in the garnering of high accolades for many of the establishments he has worked in, both in New York City and also in Estonia.

The recipes in his section are designed and were cooked using basic utensils for ease and simplicity in the home kitchen.

Poached Shrimp in Cauliflower Cream Sauce

Servings: 1 | Prep time: 25 mins | Cook time: 10 mins

EOC
~16mg

INGREDIENTS

- 5 large shrimp
- 1 small head cauliflower
- 3-4 cloves garlic, cut in half
- 1½ cups heavy cream
- 1½ cups milk

- ½ Tbsp + 2 Tbsp butter
- 2-3 fresh dill stalks, plus fronds for garnish
- 1 Tbsp olive oil
- 1 tsp apple cider vinegar

- ⅓ tsp Dijon mustard
- 1 pinch sugar
- 1 pinch + ½ tsp salt
- 1 small or half of a medium shallot

DIRECTIONS

1. Peel and devein shrimp if needed. Fresh or frozen will work fine. If using frozen, thaw before using.
2. Cut the shallot in half lengthwise and remove the ends. Peel, then slice the shallot into long thin strips. Place in a container with a pinch of salt mixed into the shallots. Let sit for ten minutes then gently rinse with water and let air dry.
3. Prepare cauliflower by rinsing under cold water and let dry.
4. Remove florets just at the base where it attaches to stalk using a small knife or the tip of a chef's knife.
5. Put aside the nicest looking bite size florets for poaching later on.
6. Cut larger florets down to the same size and then trim away any green leaves from the stalk. Save the cauliflower crumbs that fall off for crunchy texture in the salad.
7. Peel garlic and chop the cloves in half. Melt ½ tbsp butter in the pot and add the garlic. Roast for a few minutes, letting the garlic get some golden-brown color. It is okay if the butter browns a little as this will add a nice nutty flavor. Add the cut florets and the milk and cream. If needed, add water to bring the liquid up to just below the cauliflower. Simmer on medium heat till tender. Keep watch so the cream does not boil over.
8. Strain the florets from the liquid, keeping the liquid for poaching later. In a blender or food processor, blend the florets with 2 Tbsp butter, ½ tsp salt, the roasted garlic pieces and a few tablespoons of the poaching cream until silky smooth.
9. Keep the poaching cream on low heat so it is steaming, but not bubbling or simmering at all. Place the bite size cauliflower into the pot. After 3 minutes, add the shrimp into the pot and poach. Turn them over once after two to three minutes and cook three more minutes on the other side. If your pot is too small, poach the cauliflower first and then the shrimp last.
10. To make the vinaigrette, add the vinegar, Dijon mustard, salt, and sugar into a bowl. Slowly pour oil into the mixture, whisking continuously until all the oil is used and the vinaigrette is emulsified and not separated. If using lemon juice in place of apple cider vinegar, the same measurement is applied.
11. For the salad, combine the cauliflower crumbs, rinsed shallots, fresh dill with stems finely chopped and vinaigrette in a bowl.
12. Place the puree onto the plate, assemble the shrimp and florets at your discretion on the plate, and place the mixed salad in small amounts next to each shrimp and floret. Garnish with picked dill.

Save remaining cauliflower puree and poaching liquid for a cauliflower soup base if you wish.

Kohlrabi and Cucumber Salad With Burrata

Servings: 2 | Prep time: 25 mins

EOC
~5mg

INGREDIENTS

- 1 medium kohlrabi
- 1 cucumber
- ¼ tsp salt
- tarragon to garnish

- 1 handful arugula
- 1 piece burrata
- sunflower seeds to garnish

- vinaigrette x 2 (see recipe for Poached Shrimp in Cauliflower Cream Sauce on previous page

DIRECTIONS

1. Rinse the kohlrabi under cold water. Peel the kohlrabi using a knife by cutting the top and bottom off. Cut downwards, curving with the shape of the kohlrabi to remove the side skins. Cut the kohlrabi in half then in half again and proceed to cut it thin slices.
2. Rinse the cucumber under cold water. Cut into thin rounds.
3. Wash the arugula in cold water and pat dry.
4. Pick tarragon leaves from the stem.
5. Follow recipe for making a vinaigrette from the shrimp and cauliflower recipe and triple amounts.
6. Look for roasted and salted sunflower seed without the shell. If you cannot find any, toast some raw shelled sunflower seeds in a pan over medium heat till brown and sprinkle with salt.
7. Combine the cucumber, arugula, and kohlrabi in a bowl and pour the vinaigrette over them. Season with 2-3 pinches of salt. Mix thoroughly.
8. Cut the burrata in half and place it on the plate. Season each piece of burrata with a dash of salt. Place the salad onto the dish around the burrata. Top with the sunflower seeds and tarragon leaves.

*Omit the burrata in this recipe for a vegan variation.

Arctic Char and Rutabaga with Watercress and Grape Salad

Servings: 4 | Prep time 20 mins | Cook time: 1 hour, 40 mins

EOC
~5mg

INGREDIENTS

- 1 pound Arctic Char filet (salmon also works)
- 1 small to medium size rutabaga
- 2 twigs rosemary

- 1 tsp + 1 tsp salt
- 25 grapes
- 1 Tbsp olive oil
- 1 bunch watercress
- 1 small shallot

- vinaigrette x 3 (see recipe from shrimp and cauliflower)
- 1 handful whole mint leaves, ripping larger leaves in half

DIRECTIONS

1. Rinse the rutabaga under cold water, then peel it. Take a sheet of foil large enough to wrap around the rutabaga. Place the rutabaga in the middle. Rub down with vegetable oil, salt, and fresh rosemary. Wrap the rutabaga closed. Place into a 375°F oven. Roast for one and a half hours or till tender to the middle, checking with a cake tester or very small, but long-bladed knife.

2. Take the rutabaga out of the oven and open the foil to let cool. Once cool enough to handle, slice into random but equal size pieces. Once rutabaga is ready turn oven down to 350°F.

3. Wash watercress in cold water and pat dry. Wash grapes under cold water. Slice grapes in half-length ways. Make vinaigrette and sliced shallots from the shrimp and cauliflower recipe. Reserve some vinaigrette to drizzle over the plated and finished dish.

4. Take the arctic char filet, leaving the skin on, and season all over with salt. Drizzle with olive oil and place onto a baking sheet with foil. Bake at 350°F for 8-12 minutes depending on thickness of filet.

5. Combine watercress, grapes, mint, shallots, and toss with half the vinaigrette.

6. Break the arctic char fillet into large pieces, pulling gently away and leaving the skin behind. Place the arctic char pieces onto the plate, followed by the rutabaga chunks, and then some of the salad over top. Place remaining salad into a bowl to share. Drizzle remaining vinaigrette over plated dish.

Winter Beef Stew

Servings: 5 | Prep time: 20 mins | Cook time: 120 mins

EOC
~22mg

INGREDIENTS

- 1 pound beef top round
- 1 twig rosemary
- 6 cups beef stock
- 6 ounces button mushrooms, sliced thick
- 1½ cup white onions
- 5 garlic cloves
- 2 bay leaves
- 1 cup rutabaga
- 2 cups green cabbage

- 1 cup lentils
- I cup parsnip
- ¾ cup merlot red wine
- 1 tsp salt
- 2 tsp apple cider vinegar
- Chives, chopped fine for garnish
- 1 Tbsp cold water
- 1 Tbsp cornstarch

DIRECTIONS

1. Clean and peel all vegetables and cut into ½-inch diced pieces. Finely chop the garlic.
2. Remove the outer leaves of the cabbage and cut in half, removing the core. Proceed to cut the cabbage into ½-inch pieces.
3. Wash the mushrooms quickly in warm water remove any dirt. Slice thick.
4. Cut the beef into 1-inch pieces.
5. Turn heat on medium high heat and add 1 Tbsp of olive oil. Season the beef with 1 tsp of salt.
6. Fry the beef in the oil, letting it get brown without stirring. If the meat sticks, leave it to sit and caramelize and it will release naturally. Remove the beef once seared golden brown.
7. Add the mushrooms and let brown as well. Add a touch of oil if necessary. Add the vegetables except the cabbage and sweat for a few minutes. Season with a pinch of salt.
8. Add the garlic and continue to sweat, stirring frequently. Return the beef and any juice that has gathered underneath them.
9. Add the red wine and the beef stock. Reduce heat to a low simmer. Add rosemary. Let cook on low for about 1½ hours.
10. When meat is just about tender, add the lentils. Continue cooking till meat is fully tender and lentils are just becoming tender, about 15-20 minutes. Add the green cabbage.
11. Combine the cold water and cornstarch. Mix well. Add back into the stew, stirring thoroughly, and bring up to a boil for 1 to 2 minutes.
12. Taste and adjust salt and add 2 tsp apple cider vinegar.

This stew, like many, is best made a day before and reheated the following day!

Pork and Butternut Squash w/ Apple and Shiitake Mustard Sauce

Servings: 2 | Prep time: 10 mins | Cook time: 30 mins

INGREDIENTS

- 2 5.5 oz pork chops
- 4-5 shiitake mushrooms
- ½ of a granny smith apple
- ½ of one small butternut squash
- ½ Tbsp whole grain mustard

- ½-1 Tbsp olive oil
- ¼ tsp salt
- ½ tsp brown sugar
- 1 ½ Tbsp butter
- ¼ cup white wine

DIRECTIONS

1. Look for quality pork cuts, preferably from your local market or butcher. This dish can be a cinch though with prepackaged pork portions from your local grocery store as well.
2. Set oven to 375°F.
3. Rinse the butternut squash under cold water. Cut off the top stem. Cut the squash in half where the neck meets the bottom bulb. Cut in half again length ways. Reserve the bottom part for another recipe. Make cuts down into the squash just before the skin. Do the same going the other direction as to appear like scored grill marks.
4. Rub each piece of squash with ¼ tsp salt, ¼ tsp of olive oil, and ½ tsp of brown sugar. Roast in the oven for 30 minutes or until just fork tender. Having some crunchy texture to the butternut squash is ideal.
5. Clean the shiitake of any dirt with a small knife or scraping with your finger. Cut the shiitake mushrooms into six pieces, or pieces about the size of your fingertip. Cut the granny smith apple into quarters, cutting away the core from top to bottom, and then cut into the same sized pieces as the mushrooms.
6. It is not necessary to remove all fat from the pork for searing because the fat will melt and add flavor to the meat. The sauce will also be made directly after the pork in the same pan, and the mushrooms will do a fantastic job of absorbing the fat, so don't worry if you have a lot of pork fat in the pan.
7. Turn the heat under your pan to medium and let the pan get hot for one or two minutes. Add ½ tbsp of olive oil to the pan and let the oil get hot for 30 seconds. Season the pork generously with salt and place into the pan. Sear to a golden brown on both sides, turning and rotating the meat as necessary. Turn down the heat if the pan begins to smoke. Remove the pork from the pan after 4-5 minutes on each side. Let the pork sit covered with foil to retain heat. Be sure to add any liquid from the resting pork into the finished sauce.
8. Add the shiitake mushrooms to the pan and let sit for a few minutes to get browned. If needed, add ½ tbsp of oil to the pan. Stir the mushrooms and let them sit another few minutes. Add the apples and let them gain a little bit of brown color. Deglaze all the bits stuck to the pan with the white wine. Let reduce by half. Next, add the mustard and continue to stir. Take the pan off the heat and stir in your butter. Adjust for your liking with salt and if needed add a touch of water.
9. Place the squash onto one side of the plate and lay the sliced pork next to the squash. Spoon the sauce over and down one side of the pork and squash. Garnish with fresh apple slices.

Mackenzie Burgess, RDN

Recipe Blog: cheerfulchoices.com
Coaching Services: cheerfulchoices.com/coaching-and-cooking
Instagram: @cheerfulchoices

Mackenzie is a Registered Dietitian, nutritionist and recipe developer at Cheerful Choices. Her blog focuses on simple recipes with customizable ingredients of your choice. Mackenzie also offers a service called "Coaching + Cooking" where she provides virtual nutrition coaching and personalized cooking classes based on individual health goals. This is a great option for those looking to set actionable goals and increase their kitchen confidence. Connect with her on social media or check out her blog!

Cauliflower Risotto

Servings: 4
Prep time: 5 mins
Cook time: 20 mins

INGREDIENTS

- 1 Tbsp olive oil
- 8 ounces sliced mushrooms
- ½ white onion, diced
- 4 cloves garlic
- 1 cup frozen peas or other frozen vegetables of your choice
- 4 cups cauliflower rice
- 1 cup vegetable broth
- ½ cup parmesan cheese

DIRECTIONS

1. Heat oil in a large pot over medium heat. Add in mushrooms, onion, garlic, and sauté for 10 minutes until caramelized.
2. Add in peas, cauliflower rice, and broth. Simmer for 10 minutes until vegetable broth reduces slightly.
3. Turn off heat and stir in parmesan cheese.

EOC
~8mg

Honey Soy Glazed Salmon

Servings: 4 | Prep time: 10 mins
Cook time: 20 mins

EOC
~9mg

INGREDIENTS

- ¼ cup honey
- ¼ cup low sodium soy sauce or tamari
  if gluten-free
- 1 Tbsp rice vinegar
- 2 tsp grated fresh ginger
- 2 tsp grated fresh garlic, about 2 cloves
- 4, 4-ounce salmon fillets or 1 pound salmon whole
- Salt to taste
- 1 Tbsp olive oil
- Cooked jasmine rice, for serving

DIRECTIONS

1. To prepare the glaze, whisk together the honey, soy sauce, rice vinegar, ginger, and garlic in a small saucepan until well combined (*see note for optional marinating instructions).
2. Cook over medium heat, stirring often, until glaze is slightly thickened and reduced, about 5-7 minutes.
3. *To cook salmon on stovetop:* Heat olive oil in a large skillet over medium-high heat. Add the salmon to the pan, skin-side down. Cook 4-5 minutes each side or until fish flakes easily with a fork.
   To cook salmon on the grill: Rub olive oil over the fillets, making sure they are well oiled. Then, add your salmon filets, skinless side over the grill. This ensures you get those delicious grill marks. Cook for about 4-5 minutes each side or until fish flakes easily with a fork. Alternatively, you can wrap the salmon in foil and cook for 10-12 minutes until done.
   To cook salmon in the oven: Preheat oven to 425°F. Place salmon on a baking sheet and cook for 8-12 minutes, depending on the thickness and size of your fillet, until fish flakes easily with a fork.
4. Spoon soy glaze over cooked salmon filets and serve over jasmine rice, if desired.

For extra flavor, you can also marinate your salmon in the glaze ingredients for 15 minutes before transferring any leftover marinade to a small saucepan to heat and make your thickened glaze.

Chickpea "Chicken" Salad

Servings: 4
Prep Time: 10 mins

INGREDIENTS

- 1 15-oz can chickpeas
- 1 small ripe avocado, seeded and peeled
- ¼ cup light mayonnaise
- 1 cup add-ins of your choice, chopped into small pea-sized pieces (grapes, apples, red onion, red pepper, cucumber, cilantro, dill, or a combination)
- 1 Tbsp lime juice or lemon juice
- ½ tsp kosher salt

DIRECTIONS

1. In a medium sized bowl, mash together chickpeas and avocado until mostly broken down, with some larger pieces left.
2. Stir in mayonnaise, add-ins of your choice, lime or lemon juice, salt, and mix until combined. Taste and adjust spices to your liking.
3. Serve chickpea salad over mixed greens, lettuce wraps, or enjoy by itself.

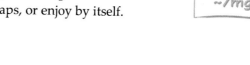

EOC
~7mg

Flaxseed Berry Jam

Servings: 3
Prep time: 5 mins

INGREDIENTS

- 1 cup fresh or frozen strawberries or blueberries
- 1 tablespoon ground flax seeds

DIRECTIONS

1. Add berries into a microwave safe bowl and microwave for 1-2 minutes until fruit is softened and starts to release some of its juices. Alternatively, you can heat the berries in a small saucepan over medium heat for about 10 minutes.
2. After heated, mash berries with a fork until fruit is mostly broken down, with some chunks left.
3. Stir in ground flax seeds and let mixture set in the fridge for 2 hours, or overnight. This allows time for the flax seeds to absorb the liquid and thicken into a jam.

EOC ~4mg
for blueberries

EOC ~7mg
for strawberries

Store any leftovers in an airtight container in the fridge for up to one week or in the freezer for up to 3 months.

Maple Roasted Squash Wedges

Servings: 6
Prep time: 10 mins
Cook time: 45 mins

INGREDIENTS

- 1 large (about 2-3 pounds) winter squash of your choice, (acorn, butternut or delicata*)
- 1 Tbsp olive oil
- 1 Tbsp maple syrup
- 1 Tbsp thyme or 1 tsp dried thyme, plus more for garnish
- ½ tsp salt

DIRECTIONS

1. Preheat oven to 400°F. Cut squash into wedges. Toss squash wedges with olive oil, maple syrup, thyme, and salt.
2. Place squash wedges on a large baking sheet lined with parchment paper and place baking sheet in the middle rack of the oven.
3. Roast for 20 minutes, then flip squash over and roast for another 20 minutes. Then, move the baking sheet to the top rack and broil squash on high for 1-2 minutes to caramelize the tops.
4. Remove from the oven and enjoy warm.
5. Store any leftovers in an airtight container in the fridge for up to 4 days.

If you are using delicata squash, you will want to use two of these since they are a smaller squash.

EOC
~4mg

Melanie Betz
MS, RD, CSR, CSG

thekidneydietitian.org
IG: @the.kidney.dietitian
TW: thekidneyrd
pinterest.com/thekidneydietitian
facebook.com/thekidneyrd

Melanie has been a Registered Dietitian for 10 years and is certified in kidney and geriatric nutrition. She is passionate about helping people with kidney stones and Chronic Kidney Disease understand that healthy eating does not have to be complicated and can be delicious!

She works at the University of Chicago and her research interests include ways to increase patient knowledge and adherence to healthy eating, frailty, and plant-based diets. Melanie also volunteers with the National Kidney Foundation of Illinois and the Healthy Aging Dietetic Practice Group.

In her free time, she enjoys cooking, yoga, wine tasting and cheering on her Michigan State Spartans!

* Catch *Melanie on Episodes 5 and 6 of the Low Oxalate Kitchen Podcast!*

Tzatziki Sauce

Servings: 8
Prep time: 10 mins

INGREDIENTS

- ½ large cucumber
- 1 ½ cups plain, low-fat yogurt
- 2 Tbsp olive oil
- 1 Tbsp white vinegar
- 2 garlic cloves, minced
- 1 tsp dried dill
- ¼ tsp salt

DIRECTIONS

1. Shred cucumber using a large tread grater. Dry shredded cucumber using paper towels. Make sure to get as much liquid as possible out of the cucumber, or your tzatziki will be watery!
2. Combine cucumber with yogurt, oil, vinegar, garlic, dill and salt. Mix well until combined.

Tzatziki is delicious to eat right away, but is even better the next day!

EOC
~1mg

Paneer Cheese

Servings: 8-12
Prep time: 2 hours

INGREDIENTS

- ½ gallon whole milk
- ¼ cup distilled vinegar (or lemon juice)
- ½ tsp salt

DIRECTIONS

1. Pour milk into a large saucepan. Warm the milk, stirring occasionally. You do not want the milk to get warmer than 200°F.
2. Add vinegar (or lemon juice) and stir to combine. The milk will begin to curdle immediately. Let the mixture sit for about 10 minutes.
3. Line a strainer with cheesecloth. Carefully pour the curdled milk over the cheesecloth, catching all the curds.
4. Collect the cheese curds in the cheesecloth and squeeze out as much of the liquid as you can. You may have to let the cheese cool before you can handle it!
5. Place the curds (in the cheesecloth) on a large plate. Sprinkle with salt. Gently press the curds into a rough 6-inch square.
6. Place another plate on top of the cheese. Put something heavy on top of the plate such as 2 cartons of broth, or a large 32oz can.
7. Let the cheese sit for 30-60 minutes. Use immediately or wrap in plastic wrap and refrigerate for up to 3 days. Enjoy!

EOC
~1mg

Salmon with Creamy Horseradish Sauce

Servings: 4
Prep time: 10 mins
Cook time: 10 mins

INGREDIENTS

- 4, 4oz salmon fillets
- Dash salt
- ¼ cup low-fat sour cream
- ¼ cup fat-free plain yogurt
- 1 Tbsp onion, minced
- 1 tsp fresh lemon juice
- 2 tsp (or more!) prepared horseradish
- 1 garlic clove, minced
- Lemon slices, for garnish

DIRECTIONS

1. Spray a baking sheet with non-stick cooking spray. Place salmon on baking sheet and sprinkle with salt. Bake 8-10 minutes at 375°F, or until fish flakes easily with a fork.
2. While fish is cooking, combine remaining ingredients to make sauce.
3. Serve salmon topped with ¼ cup horseradish sauce and lemon slices.

EOC
~1mg

Brussels Sprouts Salad

Servings: 4 | Prep time: 15 minutes

INGREDIENTS

Dressing
- ¾ cup plain, low-fat yogurt
- 1 Tbsp Dijon mustard
- 2 Tbsp maple syrup
- 1 Tbsp apple cider vinegar

Salad
- 8 ounces Brussels sprouts, shredded
- 1 apple, diced
- ¼ red onion, minced
- ½ cup fresh parsley, chopped
- 2 Tbsp blue cheese, crumbled
- ¼ cup unsalted pumpkin seeds

DIRECTIONS

1. Whisk all dressing ingredients together.
2. In a large bowl, combine all salad ingredients.
3. Toss to combine with dressing.

EOC
~10mg

Red Pepper Sauce

Servings: 5
Prep time: 10 mins
Cook time: 30 mins

INGREDIENTS

- 3 large red bell peppers
- 5 Tbsp Parmesan cheese, shredded
- 12 leaves fresh basil
- 2 cloves garlic
- ½ lemon, juiced
- 2 Tbsp olive oil
- 1 tsp red wine vinegar

PREPARATION

1. Slice peppers in half lengthwise and remove stem and seeds. Place on baking sheet and bake at 400°F for 30 minutes, rotating pan halfway through baking.
2. Let peppers cool a few minutes and then peel the skin off of them. The skin should be slightly charred and come off easily. If not, roast them for a few more minutes. It is okay if you do not get all of the skin off!
3. Combine peeled & roasted peppers with remaining ingredients in a food processor. Blend until smooth, about 1 minute. Serve immediately!

EOC ~7mg

Melissa Conover, RD

www.EnergizeNutritionRD.com
mconovernutrition@gmail.com
IG: @energizenutrition.withmelissa

Hello, my name is Melissa Conover! I am a Registered Dietitian and have been in the nutrition industry for over 10 years. I have had clinical, community, and food service experience working with clients in many areas of nutrition and dietetics.

My expertise ranges from a grocery store setting with different medical conditions and food requirements, to sports and performance nutrition, as well as customized coaching in my online business. A fun fact that many do not know - I worked at a UFC Gym owned by professional MMA fighter Frankie Edgar, where I created a nutrition program for members.

A variety of experiences and education over the years has allowed me to work with clients using a whole-life approach to wellness. I like to focus on connecting the "why" with the "how" behind nutrition, in order to optimally fuel, rather than restrict intake.

I currently work full time in my private nutrition coaching program done exclusively virtually, so I can work with clients anywhere!

Cilantro-Lime Ahi Seared Tuna over Rice Noodles

Servings: 4
Prep time: 20 mins
Cook time: 10 mins

INGREDIENTS

- 1 pound seared ahi tuna
- 1 8-ounce box rice noodles
- 1 Tbsp of avocado oil or avocado oil spray

Cilantro Lime dressing/marinade

- 2 tsp sesame oil
- 4 tsp avocado oil
- 2 Tbsp lime juice
- 2 Tbsp fresh cilantro, minced
- 2 tsp fresh ginger, minced
- 2 tsp honey
- 2 cloves garlic
- 2 Tbsp minced jalapeno
- 2 tsp low sodium soy sauce

DIRECTIONS

1. In a bowl, combine ingredients for the dressing.
2. Transfer half the cilantro dressing mix into a Ziploc bag, and leave the other half in the bowl.
3. In a large pot, bring water to a boil. Add pasta to pot and stir immediately.
4. Cook pasta for 3-4 minutes, then drain.
5. Pour small portion of dressing from reserved dressing to prevent pasta from sticking and save the rest to pour over completed dish.
6. Place the tuna into the prepared Ziploc bag. Seal, and coat with dressing mix.
7. Coat pan with 1 Tbsp avocado oil, or avocado oil spray in non-stick medium skillet (or cast-iron skillet).
8. If using non-stick pan, heat for about 1 minute on medium-high heat OR if using a cast-iron skillet allow to heat for 3-5 minutes on medium-high heat.
9. Sear the tuna (3 minutes on each side for medium, 2 minutes for medium-rare (Note: each stove may be different - adjust heat and cooking time according to your desired temperature).
10. Take the tuna off and place on cutting board to cool for about 3 minutes.
11. Slice tuna and add on top of the portioned-out noodles, with the remainder of the dressing from the bowl.

EOC
~5mg

71

Crockpot Buffalo Chicken Dip

Servings: 8 | Prep time: 10 mins | Cook time: 3-4 hours on high or 5-6 hours on low

INGREDIENTS

- 1 pound chicken breasts, boneless
- ½ cup Frank's Red-hot sauce
- 1 cup 2% cottage cheese
- 1 cup parmesan cheese
- 1 cup cheddar
- 1 cup non-fat plain Greek yogurt

Ranch spice mix*
- ½ tsp dried parsley
- ½ tsp garlic powder
- ½ tsp onion powder
- 1 tsp dill weed
- ½ tsp chives

- ¼ tsp dried minced onions

Optional
- ¼ tsp Himalayan salt
- ¼ tsp white ground pepper

EOC
~2mg

DIRECTIONS

1. Place 1 pound chicken in a Crockpot.
2. In a bowl, hand mix in the 1 cup yogurt and 3 cheeses together.
3. Pour the mixture over the chicken, and then pour in the ½ cup hot sauce.
4. Cook for 3-4 hours on high or 5-6 hours on low (ensure the chicken reaches an internal temperature of 165°F). Crockpot settings vary, so adjust accordingly.
5. Shred the chicken and mix all ingredients together. Enjoy with cucumbers, cauliflower, or your favorite chips.

*4x the ranch spice mix to have enough left over for the One Pan "Ranch Spice" Porkchop recipe on the next page!

One Pan "Ranch Spice" Porkchop

Servings: 6
Prep time: 15 mins
Cook time: 30 mins

INGREDIENTS

- 6 center-cut boneless porkchops (not thin sliced - if thin sliced, cook meat last and use 8 thin cut)
- 2-3 parsnips (depends on size)
- 1 bunch of asparagus

Ranch spice mix

- ¾ tsp dried minced onions
- ¾ tsp white pepper
- ¾ tsp Himalayan salt or sea salt
- 1 ½ tsp dried parsley
- 1 ½ tsp dried garlic powder
- 1 ½ tsp dried onion powder
- 1 Tbsp dill weed
- 1 ½ tsp dried chives

DIRECTIONS

1. Preheat oven to 375°F.
2. Cut parsnips into ½ inch thick piece "fries".
3. Cut off asparagus ends.
4. Fill a large bowl with cold water and ice and place a strainer in the sink.
5. In two separate large saucepans, boil water.
6. Parboil asparagus and parsnips separately, 30 seconds for thin pieces, and up to 2-3 minutes for thick spears/pieces.
7. Drain and immediately plunge into the ice bath to cool and stop the cooking process.
8. In a bowl, mix 7 tbsp of olive oil with ranch spice mix.
9. Divide this mix into thirds.
10. Toss ⅓ portion of oil seasoning mix with parsnips in a Ziploc or bowl.
11. Toss ⅓ oil seasoning mix with asparagus in another bowl or Ziploc.
12. In a separate bag or bowl, mix the remaining ⅓ portion with the porkchops.
13. Section the pan into thirds to place asparagus, porkchop. and parsnips.
14. Cook 30 mins or until pork reaches internal temp of 145°F and veggies are tender when you stick a fork in it.

EOC
~17mg

Coconut Chickpea Coated Mahi-Mahi in Mango Sauce

Servings: 4 | Prep time: 30 mins | Cook time: 12-15 mins

INGREDIENTS

- 4 mahi filets (4-6 oz each)
- 2 eggs
- 1 cup chickpea flour
- ½ cup unsweetened shredded coconut

Chickpea crumbs

- 1 can garbanzo beans to make homemade crumbs OR pre-made store brand "Wat-U-See Foods" chickpea crumbs

Mango sauce

- 2 mangoes or ~2 cups, pitted, peeled, and coarsely chopped
- ¼ cup lime juice
- 3 Tbsp finely chopped jalapeno
- ½ tsp salt
- 2 large garlic cloves, finely chopped
- 2 Tbsp cilantro finely chopped (optional)

DIRECTIONS

Homemade Chickpea Crumbs: (Note: if buying pre-made chickpea crumbs, skip these steps)

EOC
~11mg

1. Heat oven to 350°F.
2. Take 1 can garbanzo beans and drain.
3. Pulse in food processor until chopped (not pureed).
4. Place on parchment paper & bake 15 minutes.
5. Place in food processor again until in crumbs (not full pureed or as a sauce).
6. Put back in oven for another 15 minutes, then turn off the oven and leave the pan in until the oven cools to get rid of any excess moisture.

Mango Sauce

1. Combine all mango sauce ingredients except cilantro.
2. Combine in the food processer until made into a thick smooth puree (do not over process to full liquid).

Mahi-Mahi Dish

1. Turn up oven to 400°F.
2. In one bowl or plate, place 1 cup chickpea flour. Whisk 2 eggs in another bowl and, in a third bowl or plate, place a combination of ½ cup of chickpea crumbs with ½ cup coconut shreds. Mix together.
3. Place mahi in coconut flour first, coating both sides. Tap off excess very well.
4. Place in egg dish and flip to cover both sides.
5. Then place in coconut chickpea mixture and flip until completely covered on all sides.
6. Place on baking sheet.
7. Repeat process with each filet until all pieces are covered in the crust.
8. Bake at 400°F for 13-15 minutes, or until it flakes easy with a fork. Do not overcook.
9. Top with mango sauce, and optional chopped cilantro, and enjoy with your favorite side dish!

Mini Strawberry Cheesecakes

Servings: 18-24 | Prep time: 60 mins | Cook time: 15-20 mins

EOC ~6mg

INGREDIENTS

- ¾ cup strawberries, thinly sliced
- 12 ounces/1.5 packages cream cheese
- ¼ cup ricotta
- 2 eggs
- ¾ cups sugar
- 1 tsp vanilla extract

Chickpea crust

- 1.5 cups chickpea flour
- 1 Tbsp maple syrup
- 4.5 Tbsp softened butter
- ½ tsp Himalayan salt or sea salt
- 3 Tbsp cold water

Strawberry topping

- 4 cups strawberries
- ¼ cup cornstarch
- 1 ⅓ cup water
- 1 cup sugar
- 1 tsp vanilla extract (optional)

DIRECTIONS

1. Preheat oven to 350°F and line cupcake pans with about 18-24 cupcake liners.
2. In a medium bowl, mix 1.5 cups chickpea flour with ½ tsp salt. Add the 4.5 Tbsp softened butter, 1 Tbsp maple syrup, and water.
3. With your hands, work the butter into the flour mixture. You cannot overmix.
4. Loosely cover in plastic wrap and freeze for 20 minutes.
5. Using a hand mixer, in another medium bowl mix the 1.5 packages (12oz) cream cheese with ¼ cup (4oz) ricotta cheese and the 1 tsp vanilla. Then, mix in ¾ cups of sugar for baking, and slowly add the eggs. Hand mix this until smooth and creamy, or about 1-2 minutes total. Add in ¾ cup thinly sliced strawberries.
6. Take dough out of freezer and use a little over 1 tsp of dough to press into the bottom of cupcake liners.
7. Pour batter evenly over crust, leaving about ⅓ of space in the liner, and bake at 350°F for 18-20 minutes.
8. For the topping, combine all strawberry topping ingredients in a medium saucepan.
9. Turn stove on medium-high heat and stir frequently until thick and clear.
10. Once cheesecakes are cool, pour 1-2 Tbsp of strawberry mixture over top and refrigerate for minimum 1 hour.

Patrick Carty

Instagram: @pc_nutr
linkedin.com/in/patrick19carty

Patrick is a graduate of Penn State University, where he earned his Bachelor's Degree in Nutritional Sciences. Healthy living, combined with balanced nutrition, has always been his mantra, starting way back in his younger days. He enjoys sharing his passion with others, and especially loves how the right foods can feed the body both internally and externally. Patrick also enjoys modifying kitchen recipes and "creating something from nothing", using whatever is on hand to make a deliciously and nutritiously satisfying meal!

Patrick's goal is to put an innovative spin on any recipe so that you never get bored, all while keeping good nutrition in mind. His hope is to educate and inspire others to find that eating healthy does not have to be expensive or complicated, and he believes that everyone can enjoy the simple pleasures of preparing and eating food made with healthy ingredients. Patrick aspires to be a personal chef/nutritionist, so that he can pass along his knowledge and love of food to his clients.

He is currently in the process of becoming a health coach. You can check out his Instagram for new and exciting recipes and tips on eating healthy, and you can also connect with him on LinkedIn!

77

Butternut Squash Pancakes

Yield: 12 4-inch pancakes

Servings: 4
Prep time: 15 mins
Cook time: 20 mins for
frozen squash, 45 mins for
fresh squash

INGREDIENTS

- 3 cups butternut
  squash puree
- ½ cup water
- ½ cup white rice flour
- ½ tsp real vanilla
  extract
- 2 large eggs
- 1 Tbsp baking powder
- ½ tsp cardamom
- 1 pinch of salt

Filling:
- 1 cup
  ricotta
- ¼ cup confectionary sugar

DIRECTIONS

1. You can use fresh or frozen butternut squash. If using fresh, cut in half and remove seeds. Season with 1 tsp of salt divided evenly between the two halves. Roast in oven at 400°F for 30-40 minutes until squash is golden brown and tender with the poke of a fork.
2. If using frozen diced butternut squash, cook in pan on medium heat for 5-10 minutes, season with 1 tsp of salt. Cook until soft enough to puree.
3. Puree the squash with the water in a food processor. Transfer to a large bowl.
4. Then, lightly mix in the rest of the ingredients and seasoning with additional salt to taste. Don't overmix the batter as it can become tough. Use a spatula to do this.
5. Heat up large frying pan with baking spray or butter. Let the pan get hot enough before adding batter at a medium heat.
6. Add in ¼ cup of batter in at a time. This will yield a 3.5-4 inch pancake. Cook on one side for a minute or two, then flip over and cook for an additional minute or two.
7. In a small separate bowl, combine ricotta and confectionary sugar for pancake filling. Mix until combined, spoon on top of pancakes.

Balsamic Glazed Meatloaf

Servings: 8
Prep time: 10 mins
Cook time: 40 mins

INGREDIENTS

- 2 pounds ground beef, 85%-90% lean
- 2 eggs
- 3 cloves garlic
- 3 Tbsp parsley
- 2 tsp paprika
- ½ tsp dried thyme
- ⅓ cup milk
- 1 tsp salt
- ¼ tsp white pepper
- ½ tsp paprika

Sauce

- ¼ cup brown sugar
- 2 Tbsp balsamic vinegar

DIRECTIONS

1. Preheat oven to 375°F.
2. In a large bowl, combine all ingredients for the meatloaf. Mix well.
3. Line a baking sheet with foil and form the mixture into a loaf with your hands.
4. Bake for 40 minutes, adding sauce in step 5 halfway through cooking.
5. In separate bowl, combine brown sugar and balsamic vinegar, pour mixture over meatloaf 20 minutes into cooking.
6. Take out of oven, slice and serve.

EOC
~3mg

Paprika Encrusted Shrimp Tacos

Servings: 4
Prep time: 30 mins
Cook time: 10 mins

INGREDIENTS

- 1 pound large, deveined shrimp
- 2-3 cups shredded green cabbage
- ½ cup red cabbage
- 1 carrot, julienned/strips
- 8 jicama tortillas

Lime Sauce

- ¼ cup of olive oil
- Juice of 2 limes
- ½ cup plain Greek yogurt
- ½ tsp of salt
- 2 cloves of garlic, diced
- ½ cup of cilantro

Taco spice mix

- ¼ tsp cayenne pepper
- 1 tsp salt
- 1 tsp paprika
- ½ tsp onion powder
- ½ tsp garlic powder

DIRECTIONS

1. Defrost deveined shrimp in strainer under cold water for 10-20 minutes.
2. Bring a small pot of water to a boil.
3. Add lime sauce ingredients into a food processor and blend until smooth. Toss shredded cabbage with sauce until coated. Set some aside for topping.
4. Add carrot to pot of boiling water and cook for 5 mins. Strain and set aside as topping for tacos.
5. Combine all taco spice ingredients into a small bowl, stir until mixed.
6. Pat shrimp dry of water from the strainer, then coat shrimp in taco spice mixture in bowl
7. Heat drizzle of oil in pan over medium heat and sauté for 5-8 minutes, flipping occasionally, until the shrimp are cooked through.
8. Divide shrimp amongst 8 tortillas, then layer with cabbage slaw mixture. To finish, top with carrot strips and additional sauce as desired. Enjoy!

EOC
~11mg

Chicken Escarole Pasta

Servings: 6
Prep time: 10 mins
Cook time: 25 mins

INGREDIENTS

- 1 pound ground chicken
- 1 pound box of chickpea bowtie pasta
- 3 cups of escarole
- 1 large shallot
- 2 Tbsp of olive oil
- 1 tsp of thyme
- 3 cloves of garlic, minced
- 15 ounce can of chickpeas
- Salt & white pepper to taste

DIRECTIONS

1. Boil large pot of water for pasta, season with salt.
2. Finely chop shallot and sauté with oil in pan with ground chicken until brown.
3. Add pasta to boiling water.
4. Once chicken is cooked, add garlic, escarole, thyme, and chickpeas. Sauté until escarole is wilted and all ingredients are warmed.
5. Strain pasta, combine with chicken mixture, stir, and enjoy.

EOC ~21mg

Vegetarian Stuffed Peppers

Servings: 6 | Prep time: 25 mins | Cook time: 35 mins

EOC
~17mg

INGREDIENTS

- 1 cup diced onions
- 1 ½ cups of Fuji apples
- 1 cup shitake mushrooms
- 1 cup of rice
- 2 tsp dried thyme
- 1 tsp dried sage
- ½ tsp salt
- 2 Tbsp Olive oil
- 1 tsp white pepper
- ½ cup pumpkin seeds
- 6 medium bell peppers

DIRECTIONS

1. Preheat oven to 350°F.
2. Bring 2 cups of water to a boil for rice, season with salt. Add thyme and sage to water when cooking.
3. Meanwhile, heat olive oil in large skillet over medium heat. Sauté onions, apples, mushrooms and salt and pepper until softened. Combine cooked rice with vegetable/apple mixture and mix until combined. Stir in pumpkin seeds.
4. Core and seed 6 bell peppers, just cutting off the top of the pepper to be able to stuff.
5. Spoon rice mixture into peppers until filled.
6. Bake for 30-35 minutes until peppers are tender and rice mixture is heated through.

Rochelle Ramos

IG: @rockaeramos

Blogs:
rochelleramos.500px.photography
azeiteandazulejos.com

Rochelle is an Americana living life in the Portuguese countryside where she cooks up recipes and captures photos with the intent to whet the appetite and inspire the hungry.

While dabbling fairly seriously in Portuguese cooking, it is not the only cuisine that she is influenced by. Growing up in the Pacific Northwest corner of the US gave her the chance to sample an assortment of food cultures and made her crave the chance to try new and exciting fare, be it only through taste or with hands on experience.

When she's not taking part in rural life at home, she can usually be found wandering around Portugal and its old-world cities with her camera or savoring the seasonal fare, but more often than not, both!

Arroz de Grelos – Rice with Turnip Greens

Servings: 4 | Prep time: 10 mins | Cook time: 40 mins

INGREDIENTS

- 7 ounces turnip greens
- 5 garlic cloves
- 1 medium onion
- 3 Tbsp olive oil
- 1 cup rice
- 2 cups water
- 1 ½ Tbsp white wine vinegar
- coarse salt

EOC
~12mg

DIRECTIONS

1. Wash the turnip greens under cool water to remove any dirt. Trim the ends and discard them before roughly chopping the leaves. Peel the onion and garlic and mince both.
2. Heat the olive oil in a large sauté pan over medium-high heat. Add the garlic and onion to the pan and sauté 3-4 minutes. Reduce the heat to medium-low and add the turnip greens to the pan, stirring to combine, and cover with a lid. Allow the greens to wilt and the stems to soften, stirring occasionally; about 7-9 minutes.
3. Remove the lid and add the rice to the pan. Stir the rice into the greens and add ¼ of the water, stirring. Let the rice cook, absorbing some of the water, before adding in the rest of the water.
4. Let the rice continue to cook, stirring occasionally. Once the rice has finished cooking through, turn off the heat. The texture should be more creamy than dry.
5. Add the vinegar and season with salt to taste, cover and let it sit 5-10 minutes before serving.

Bolos de Arroz – Portuguese Rice Cakes

Servings: 8
Prep time: 20 mins
Cook time: 20 mins

INGREDIENTS

- butter for greasing
- 1 ⅓ cup rice flour
- 1 tsp baking powder
- ¼ tsp salt
- ⅓ cup butter, softened
- ⅔ cup sugar
- 3 eggs
- 1 lemon, juiced

DIRECTIONS

EOC
~3mg

1. Preheat the oven to 350°F and line a muffin tin with paper muffin cups.
2. Whisk the rice flour, baking powder, and salt in a bowl and set aside.
3. In a clean bowl, cream the sugar and butter together with an electric mixer until well blended. Add the eggs one a time, incorporating before adding the next. Add the lemon and mix well. Stir the flour mix into the butter and sugar mixture well with a wooden spoon.
4. Fill 8 muffin cups with the batter to the top. Bake the rice cakes in the oven for 20 minutes, or until they have risen, and a toothpick inserted in the middle comes out clean. Remove the cakes from the oven and sprinkle with a little sugar on top of each.
5. Allow the rice cakes to cool 10 minutes before removing them from the tin. Serve warm or at room temperature.

Sapateira Recheada – Portuguese Style Crab Dip

Servings: 4 | Prep time: 15 mins

INGREDIENTS

- 1 cooked brown crab
- 1 shallot, minced
- 1 hard-boiled egg, finely chopped
- 2 tsp capers, minced
- 2 Tbsp mayonnaise
- 1 Tbsp beer
- 1 tsp mustard
- ½ tsp paprika
- salt
- fresh parsley leaves

DIRECTIONS

1. Remove the meat from the crab by taking hold of the claws close to where they are attached to the body, twist and pull to remove them. Repeat with the legs and set them aside. Turn the crab over onto its back so that its belly is up and a triangular piece is attached. Fit a knife in the line at the back of the crab, opposite of the mouth, and carefully pry it up. Remove this, and the feathery looking gills, discarding them.
2. Scoop out any meat and orange roe that is inside the body of the crab and transfer it to a bowl. Wash the inside and outside of the shell of the body thoroughly and set it aside.
3. Crack the shell on the legs and claws with a nutcracker or mallet and remove the meat, adding it to the bowl with the other meat.
4. Add the shallot, egg, capers, mayonnaise, beer, mustard, paprika, and salt to taste. Spoon the crab mixture into the reserved shell along with parsley leaves.
5. Serve immediately or cover and refrigerate until ready to serve.

Fried Coconut Prawns with Honey Cream Sauce

Servings: 4 | Prep time: 15 mins | Cook time: 10 mins

EOC
~4mg

INGREDIENTS

- 1 pound raw prawns, rinsed, peeled and deveined
- ½ cup coconut flour
- ½ cup corn starch
- 1 cup shredded coconut
- 1 tsp salt
- ½ tsp white pepper
- 2 eggs, beaten
- canola oil
- 2 Tbsp Greek yogurt
- 2 Tbsp mayonnaise
- 2 Tbsp honey
- 1 Tbsp cream
- green onion for garnish
- salt

DIRECTIONS

1. Pour 2-3 inches of oil into a deep heavy bottomed pan and heat it to 350°F over medium-high heat.
2. Mix the coconut flour, cornstarch, salt, and white pepper in a bowl. Pour the shredded coconut into another bowl and the eggs into a third bowl.
3. Dip the prawns, one at a time, in the egg wash, then to the flour mixture, back into the egg, then into the shredded coconut and lay it on a clean plate.
4. Once the oil is hot, add the prawns to the pan in batches. Fry the prawns until they have turned pink and have curled into a "C" shape. Transfer the cooked prawns to a paper towel lined plate to drain of excess oil and sprinkle them with salt while still hot.
5. Stir the yogurt, mayonnaise, honey, cream, and onion in a bowl. Season with salt to taste. Reserve the green onion tops for serving.
6. Serve the fried coconut prawns with the honey cream sauce and green onion tops while still hot.

Eggs Royale on Portobello Mushrooms

Servings: 2 | Prep time: 35 mins | Cook time:

INGREDIENTS

- 4 ounces smoked salmon

For Onions

- 1 red onion, peeled and thinly sliced
- ¾ cup white vinegar
- 1 tsp salt
- ½ tsp sugar

Hollandaise Sauce

- 1½ cup butter, warmed
- water
- 2 medium egg yolks
- ½ Tbsp cold water
- ½ lemon, juiced
- salt
- white pepper

For Mushrooms

- 2 large portobello mushrooms, stem removed
- 3 Tbsp olive oil

Poached Eggs

- 1-2 Tbsp white vinegar
- 2 egg

DIRECTIONS

1. Place the sliced red onion in a bowl and add the vinegar, salt, and sugar and stir. Cover and set aside for at least 15 minutes.
2. To make the hollandaise, melt the butter in a small sauce pan over low heat. Allow the butter to simmer until no more foam forms on top. Turn off the heat, skim the foam off the clarified butter and discard it.
3. Bring a small pot, about ⅓ of the way full of water, to a boil over high heat. Once it has come to a boil, reduce the heat to medium-low and allow the water to continue to simmer.
4. In a medium to large sized heat-proof bowl, whisk the yolks and cold water together for 1-2 minutes until frothy. Place the bowl on the pot so that it does not touch the water, but heats up the yolks, whisking continuously until it has started to thicken slightly.
5. Remove the bowl from the pot and gradually, a tablespoon or 2 at a time, whisk the warm butter into the yolks. Keep whisking until all of the butter has been incorporated. Whisk the lemon juice into the sauce and season with salt and white pepper. Keep whisking until the sauce has thickened. Cover to keep warm and set aside.
6. Heat the olive oil in a large sauté pan over medium-high heat. Lay the portobello mushrooms, cap side down. Cook for 4-5 minutes on each side until browned and tender. Season with salt to taste and transfer to a plate lined with paper towels.
7. To poach the eggs, bring a pot filled with 3-4 inches of water and the vinegar in a small pot to a simmer over medium-high heat. As soon as it has started to simmer, reduce the heat to medium-low.
8. Carefully crack the eggs into individual ramekins. Once the water has quit simmering, and while very hot, stir the water to create a whirlpool. Drop one egg into the water and allow it to cook 3 minutes. Using a slotted spoon, remove the egg from the pot and gently place it on a paper towel lined plate to drain off excess water. Repeat with the other egg.
9. Reheat the pan used to cook the mushrooms over medium heat. Return the mushrooms to the pan for 1-2 minutes, just to warm them through.
10. To assemble the eggs royale, place a portobello mushroom on the plate and top with half of the smoked salmon, one poached egg, hollandaise sauce, onion, and top with capers. Repeat with the other ingredients. Serve immediately.

EOC ~9mg

Stacey Isaacs

kitchenofyouth.com
theharvestinnnofo.com

My name is Stacey Isaacs. I am the writer and creator of Kitchen Of Youth. I have had many careers. I've been a chef, a lawyer, and a writer/editor. I also have a Master's degree in Oriental Medicine/Herbs and a license in Acupuncture. Some people find this diversity interesting and others think I have the attention-span of a gnat.

When I was done being a lawyer (yes, I got burned out), I fulfilled a long-time fantasy and went to cooking school. This was awesome! I was lucky enough, upon graduation, to work at Food Network as a cook and food stylist. I worked with Rachel Ray, Guy Fieri, Emeril Lagasse, Bobby Flay, Tyler Florence, Mario Batalli, Cat Cora and others. This was my dream come true. But, deep in my soul, I still had the calling to be a healer.

I began cooking foods for people who had specific dietary needs. I was a personal-chef-of-sorts to people with cancer, gluten intolerance, Parkinson's, chronic fatigue syndrome, fibromyalgia, arthritis and many more conditions. I also advised, menu-planned and cooked for people who wanted to lose weight and look and feel youthful and healthy. I became an expert at healing through foods.

I've found my passion, and that is: Wellness. I love to cook delicious, chef-quality food that's good for you and easy to prepare. As a chef, I insist on using only top-quality ingredients. By top-quality, I don't necessarily mean expensive; I mean fresh, environmentally-friendly, great tasting herbs, spices, meats, vegetables, etc. As an eastern medicine practitioner, I look at foods with an eye toward their healing properties. I combine the correct foods with the correct food herbs and Chinese herbs to create a unique system to help you heal.

I am the least judgmental person on the planet, and I truly love meeting new people and celebrating all the differences between us. I concentrate my efforts on preparing chef-quality dishes that are easy for non-chefs to prepare. I combine my passion for cooking with my knowledge for whole-body-wellness by using foods, exercise, meditation, qi gong, herbs and acupuncture to heal the body, mind and spirit. I'm happy to share anything I know and all that I am still learning with anyone who is interested.

Above all, remember "it's not rocket science; it's only food." I look forward to helping you.

Stacey and her husband also run a bed and breakfast called The Harvest Inn, located in North Fork, on the northeast part of Long Island in New York. Be sure to visit if you are in the area and check out Stacey's delicious cooking in person!

Healthy Chicken Piccata

Servings: 4
Prep time: 10 mins
Cook time: 15 mins

EOC
~11mg

INGREDIENTS

- 8 boneless chicken thighs
- Salt to taste
- 1 ½ cups rice flour, or other low oxalate flour of choice
- 2 Tbsp dried, minced onion flakes
- ¼ cup ghee (you may not need this much)
- ¼ cup extra-virgin olive oil (again, you may not need this much)
- Juice of 2 lemons
- 1 large shallot, chopped
- 4 large garlic cloves, chopped
- 1 ¼ cups chicken stock or bone broth
- ¼ cup fresh parsley, chopped

INSTRUCTIONS

1. Season the chicken with salt.
2. Put the rice flour in a shallow pie plate. Add a generous amount of salt and the dried onion flakes. Stir to combine.
3. Dredge the chicken in this mixture so it's well coated.
4. Heat 2 Tbsp of ghee and 2 Tbsp oil in a large pan over medium heat. When hot, add the chicken and let brown on one side, then flip and brown on the other side, about 5-min per side. Then cover, reduce heat, and let cook for another few mins or until the chicken is cooked through.
5. Move the cooked chicken to a plate, and repeat the process with any remaining chicken.
6. When all of the chicken is done and removed from the pan, add the shallot and garlic to the pan drippings and cook, stirring, 1 min.
7. Add the capers and lemon juice to the pan. Now add the broth. Simmer for about 5 mins or until the sauce is reduced a bit.
8. Stir in 1 or 2 Tbsp of ghee and let simmer 1 min.
9. Add the chicken back into the pan, sprinkle parsley on top, and serve it right in the pan.

Cauliflower Chickpea Soup

Servings: 6 | Prep time: 10 mins | Cook time: 55 mins

INGREDIENTS

- 2 Tbsp extra-virgin olive oil
- 2 med yellow onion, roughly chopped
- 1 head cauliflower, roughly chopped

- Sea salt to taste
- ½ tsp hot red pepper flakes, or to taste
- 5 garlic cloves, smashed

- 2 16-oz cans chickpeas, drained and rinsed
- white truffle oil, to drizzle on soup when serving

EOC
~14mg

INSTRUCTIONS

1. Heat the oil in a large pot over medium heat.
2. Add the onions and garlic and cook, stirring, about 3 minutes.
3. Add cauliflower, red pepper flakes, about 2 tsp salt (or to taste).
4. Pour in 6 cups of water. Bring to a boil, then reduce the heat, cover partially, and simmer for 40 minutes.
5. Pour the soup, in 3 batches, into the blender and whiz it up until completely creamy and smooth. (I used my Vitamix and it worked great.) *NOTE: when pureeing hot liquid in blender, cover the top tightly with a clean dish towel instead of the blender lid's center insert so that the steam can release and you can stay safe!
6. As the batches are pureed, pour them into a large bowl. When all are done, transfer the soup back into the pot and add the chickpeas to the soup in the pot, and simmer for 15 minutes.
7. Ladle into bowls and drizzle a little bit of white truffle oil on top of each bowl.

Creamy Apple Cider Vinegar Chicken

Servings: 4
Prep time: 5 mins
Cook time: 30 mins

INGREDIENTS

- 1 ⅓ pounds boneless chicken thighs (about 7 thighs)
- 1 Tbsp extra-virgin olive oil
- 1 medium onion, sliced
- 4 large garlic cloves, smashed
- ⅔ cup raw apple cider vinegar
- 1 cup chicken bone broth
- 5 sprigs fresh thyme
- 1 can full-fat coconut milk (use the thick cream on the top and save the liquid for another use)

EOC
~9mg

INSTRUCTIONS

1. Heat the oil in a large skillet over medium-high heat.
2. Season the chicken with salt.
3. Add the chicken and brown on both sides.
4. Remove the cooked chicken to a plate and add the onions and garlic to the pan. Stir for 1 minute.
5. Pour in the vinegar and stir, scraping up any browned bits on the bottom of the pan.
6. Pour in the broth.
7. Put the chicken back into the pan and add the thyme sprigs.
8. Cover and simmer 20-minutes, or until it's cooked through (flipping the chicken over halfway through).
9. Remove the chicken from the pan and pour the coconut cream into the pan. Whisk until combined well and let simmer about 5 minutes, or until the sauce starts to thicken a bit.
10. Discard the thyme sprigs and serve. Enjoy!

Stephanie Boyd, RD, CDCES

Hi! My name is Steph and I LOVE food. Growing up, I was introduced to many different types of food, as my three sisters and I enjoyed my mother's home cooking throughout our childhood. We were all athletes and played competitive sports so fueling our bodies appropriately was important for both us and my parents. Our family was always big on large gatherings for birthdays, holidays, and celebrations, and you know that always included a decadent meal.

My world of nutrition was further opened when I decided to major in Nutritional Sciences at the University of Arizona and took the track to becoming a Registered Dietitian. Since becoming an RD, I have had lots of clinical experience, from working in a skilled nursing facility, to an outpatient dialysis center, to an outpatient bariatric clinic that also included patients with gastric cancer. I have also included some health coaching in my career with working at a gym doing nutrition consultations and meal planning with clients, as well as running my own small health coaching business on the side to assist people with reaching the goals they desire.

Regardless of what I have done as an RD, I have always found myself continuing to enjoy cooking and developing recipes more than anything. Myself, my family, and my friends have been involved in my own personal experience of testing with new recipes and ingredients. My husband has really enjoyed it! While I enjoy keeping my recipes healthy and clean, I also pride myself on making them taste delicious! Food is a part of our daily lives and is necessary for our body to perform its daily functions. The human body is an amazing thing and can be influenced by what you feed it. But it is also important to enjoy the food you prepare as well. I am a true believer in a healthy, realistic lifestyle that includes healthy, nutrient dense foods, as well as food that tastes flavorful and delicious. I truly believe that food and nutrition can bring out the best in people and bring happiness and joy to all!

Egg Casserole

Servings: 8
Prep time: 25 mins
Cook time: 75 mins

EOC
~11mg

INGREDIENTS

- 12 eggs
- 2 cups cottage cheese
- 1 whole Kabocha squash
- 1 red bell pepper
- 1 green bell pepper
- 1 medium yellow onion
- 8 ounces of ham
- 2 cups shredded cheddar cheese
- Salt and white pepper to taste
- Nonstick cooking spray

DIRECTIONS

1. Preheat oven to 375°F.
2. Spray a 9x12 Pyrex dish with any nonstick spray of choice.
3. Beat eggs in large bowl until yolks are completely broken and mixed in.
4. Dice all vegetables - kabocha squash, red bell pepper, green bell pepper, yellow onion. For kabocha squash, cut in half and scrape the seeds out, then dice into smaller pieces (skin can stay on). Caution: be very careful cutting the squash. It's best to cut the ends off first to have a flat surface to place the squash on.
5. Dice ham, then mix all ingredients together in large bowl (save 1 cup cheddar cheese for top of casserole).
6. Pour mixture into sprayed Pyrex dish.
7. Top with other 1 cup of cheddar cheese.
8. Bake for 1 hour and 15 minutes while covered with foil.
9. Uncover and cook additional 10 minutes if egg is not fully cooked through.
10. For serving, add more cheese if desired! This would also taste good with a dollop of sour cream or plain Greek yogurt!

Fruit and Yogurt Parfait

Servings: 1
Prep time: 10 mins
Cook time: 10 mins

INGREDIENTS

- 1 single serving cup (5.3 ounces) plain Greek yogurt
- ¼ cup diced apple of choice
- ¼ cup blueberries
- 2 Tbsp candied pumpkin seeds
- A drizzle of honey to taste

For candied pumpkin seeds (8 servings)

- nonstick cooking spray
- 2 Tbsp maple syrup
- 2 Tbsp packed brown sugar
- ¼ tsp salt
- 1 cup pepitas

DIRECTIONS

EOC
~6mg

For candied pumpkin seeds

1. Preheat oven to 375°F and oil a cookie sheet with nonstick cooking spray.
2. In a saucepan, mix the maple syrup, brown sugar, and salt. Place over medium and continue stirring until everything is combined and melted together. This will happen quickly.
3. Add in the pumpkin seeds and stir together until fully combined.
4. Spread out mixture onto the oiled cookie sheet.
5. Bake for 5 minutes, remove and stir the pumpkin seeds, then bake for another 5 minutes.
6. After 10 minutes in the oven, remove pumpkin seeds and allow to cool, making sure to mix the seeds around every so often to prevent them from sticking together.
7. Feel free to add as a topping to pretty much anything, to the parfait recipe provided, or just alone! These taste like candy!

For parfait

1. Put yogurt into a single serving bowl.
2. Dice apple of choice.
3. Sprinkle the apples and blueberries over the yogurt.
4. Sprinkle the pumpkin seeds.
5. Drizzle honey to taste.
6. Enjoy this single serving parfait! Feel free to add more of the toppings if desired!

Taco Salad

Servings: 4
Prep time: 10 mins
Cook time: 10 mins

INGREDIENTS

- 1 pound ground beef
- 1 whole yellow onion, finely chopped
- 2 cloves of garlic
- 1 Tbsp chili powder
- 1 Tbsp onion powder
- 2 tsp white pepper
- Salt to taste
- 8 cups romaine lettuce
- 8 ounces shredded cheddar cheese
- 1 cup sour cream (or plain Greek yogurt)
- Hot sauce if desired

DIRECTIONS

1. In a small bowl, mix together all of the spices.
2. Dice the onion into small pieces.
3. Cook the ground beef and onion together in a frying pan over medium high heat. Cook until beef is cooked through completely.
4. Add in the garlic and cook for a few more minutes.
5. Pour the bowl of spice mix into the fry pan and mix everything together to combine.
6. In a larger bowl, add 2 cups romaine lettuce and ¼ of the ground beef mixture.
7. Add 2 ounces of shredded cheddar cheese, ¼ cup sour cream (or Greek yogurt), hot sauce as desired.
8. Stir to combine all ingredients as desired for composed salad. Add more seasonings and toppings as desired.

EOC
~18mg

Spaghetti Squash Casserole

Servings: 4
Prep time: 15 mins
Cook time: 45 mins

EOC
~14mg

INGREDIENTS

- 1 large spaghetti squash (or 2 small spaghetti squash if you can't find large)
- 1 Tbsp minced garlic
- 1 pound ground turkey
- 1 medium yellow onion
- 1 bag of sliced mushrooms (~10 ounces)
- 1 cup mozzarella cheese
- Salt and white pepper to taste
- Scallion for garnish

DIRECTIONS

1. Preheat oven to 375°F.
2. Using a cutting board and knife, cut spaghetti squash in half and scrape the inside seeds out using a spoon. Be very careful cutting the squash in half! *Tip: cut the ends off to have a flat surface to cut it in half.*
3. Place squash on an aluminum foil lined cookie sheet, flat side down, and bake 45 minutes to an hour.
4. While spaghetti squash is in the oven, cook ground turkey over medium high heat in a pan on the stove.
5. Add salt and white pepper to taste.
6. Dice the medium yellow onion and garlic (if using fresh cloves, you can also use pre-minced garlic) into small pieces while ground turkey is cooking.
7. Once ground turkey is cooked through, put in large bowl and set to the side.
8. Place diced onion and sliced mushrooms in same pan on the stove and cook over medium high heat.
9. Add salt and white pepper to taste.
10. Add garlic towards the end of the cooking process when onions and mushrooms are cooked to liking.
11. Remove from heat and add onion, mushroom, and garlic mixture to large bowl with ground turkey.
12. Once spaghetti squash is done baking (fork tender), use a fork to scrape the inside of the squash out (should look like spaghetti noodles). *Caution: the squash will be very hot.* Use an oven mitt to hold the squash while you scrape the inside out.
13. Add squash to the large bowl with other ingredients and stir to combine completely.
14. Salt and white pepper to taste.
15. When plating, serve ¼ of ingredients, ¼ cup of mozzarella cheese, and garnish with green onion.

This also tastes good with a dollop of plain Greek yogurt as a side dipping sauce, which also adds some extra protein to the meal.

Teriyaki Ground Turkey Cauliflower Rice Bowls

Servings: 4 + extra teriyaki sauce
Prep time: 20 mins
Cook time: 30 mins

EOC ~17mg

INGREDIENTS

- 2 bags of frozen cauliflower rice (~20 ounces total)
- 2 large zucchinis
- 2 cups broccoli
- 1 bag of sliced mushrooms (~10 ounces)
- 1 pound of ground turkey
- ¼ cup teriyaki sauce
- Salt and white pepper to taste

For Teriyaki Sauce

- ¼ cup soy sauce
- ¼ cup honey
- 1 tsp ginger, grated
- 1 tsp minced garlic

DIRECTIONS

1. Preheat oven to 375°F and line a cookie sheet with aluminum foil.
2. Chop zucchini and broccoli into small pieces and add, along with sliced mushrooms, to the lined cookie sheet (or 2 sheets if needed for space).
3. Sprinkle salt and white pepper to taste, place cookie sheet(s) in oven and set a timer for 30 minutes.
4. While ingredients in the oven are cooking, place frozen cauliflower rice in a pan on the stove over medium high heat. Be sure to break up the large pieces that are still frozen together. Also, spreading out the cauliflower rice evenly throughout the whole pan allows the rice to cook faster and to get crispy parts, if desired. The goal with the frozen cauliflower rice is to cook out all of the water.
5. Add salt and white pepper to taste.
6. Allow to cook until cauliflower rice is cooked through and is browned to color of liking.
7. Place cooked cauliflower rice into a large bowl and set aside.
8. Add ground turkey in the same pan as cauliflower rice, add salt and white pepper to taste. Sauté until fully cooked through and add to same large bowl as cauliflower rice. The ground turkey and cauliflower rice should take about 30 minutes total for both to fully cook and be done by the time the vegetables in the oven are done.
9. Once vegetables in oven are done cooking, combine with cauliflower rice and ground turkey in the same bowl.
10. Whisk all 4 teriyaki sauce ingredients in small bowl, then add to other ingredients in the large bowl.
11. Stir to combine all ingredients fully and serve with a dollop of Greek yogurt.

Tejal Pathak MS, RD, LD, CDCES

tejrd.com
FB: TejRd
IG: @rdntej
rdn.tej@gmail.com

Tejal is Registered Dietitian, Certified Diabetes Care and Education Specialist, and founder of TejRD nutrition practice. She has been working in the field of dietetics for the past 12+ years and she continues to serve the profession in many areas including, but not limited to, clinical and community positions.

Along the way, Tejal has mentored many dietetic students and provided guidance to new dietitians in the field. She was also honored with the Recognized Young Dietitian of the Year award. She has been quoted in many publications like *Food Network*, *Today's Dietitian*, *Eat This, Not That!*, *ADA Times* (now known as *Food and Nutrition magazine*), *Greatist*, *The Healthy* and *EatingWell*, among others.

Her passion lies in helping others manage diabetes and cardiac health by making personalized lifestyle choices that are sustainable, budget friendly, and are simple to incorporate. Being a mom herself, she shares her experience and love while working with prenatal women, emphasizing the importance of nutrition during pregnancy. In her spare time, she creates Indian and American fusion recipes for her followers to please various cravings, and she also participates in community services by volunteering to speak about diabetes to not-for-profit organizations like SEWA International. When Tejal is not working, she enjoys hiking, biking, glacier walks and camping with her two kids and her husband.

Arugula Fruit Salad

Servings: 3 | Prep time: 10 mins

EOC
~2mg

INGREDIENTS

- 2 cups seedless chopped watermelon
- ½ cup blueberries
- ½ cup chopped arugula
- 1 Tbsp fresh lime juice
- 4 small leaves fresh mint, shredded
- ⅛ tsp fresh serrano pepper (optional)

DIRECTIONS

1. In a bowl, add watermelon, blueberries and arugula.
2. Add mint, green chili, lime juice and mix.

Optional: basil, parsley

Bottle Gourd Dessert (Dudhi Halwa)

Servings: 4 | Prep time: 15 mins | Cook time: 30 mins

INGREDIENTS

- 1 Tbsp Ghee
- 4 cups shredded bottle gourd
- ½ cup sugar
- ½ cup nonfat dry milk powder
- ½ cup 2% milk
- 2 whole cardamom pods, powdered

DIRECTIONS

1. In a pan, add ghee and let it get slightly warm. Add bottle gourd and sauté for 5-8 minutes on medium flame or until soft (you can cover the pan with a lid so it will cook faster). Stir in between to prevent from getting burnt.
2. Once bottle gourd is cooked, add milk powder and milk. Cook for another 5-8 minutes and add sugar (you may want to add ¼ cup initially and add remaining later to control sweetness).
3. Cook for an additional 10-12 minutes, stirring in between, or until all liquid dries up and mixture starts coming together. Taste for sweetness and, if desired, add remaining ¼ cup sugar. Continue to cook for 5-8 minutes more or until liquid is evaporated.
4. Add cardamom powder and mix. This dessert tastes best when warm but can be served cold as well.

Sprouted Mung Bean Salad

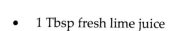

Servings: 3

Prep time: 10 mins, + sprouting time if making your own sprouts

Cook time: 15-20 mins

INGREDIENTS

- 2 cups mung bean sprouts (or 2 cups of mung beans to sprout your own)
- 1 small clove garlic, shredded
- ¼ cup chopped green onion
- ¼ cup chopped red onion
- ½ serrano pepper, shredded
- ¼ tsp fresh ginger paste
- ¼ tsp salt
- 1 Tbsp fresh lime juice
- 1 Tbsp cooking oil
- 1 Tbsp chopped cilantro (optional)

EOC
~14mg

DIRECTIONS

To make Mung Bean Sprouts

1. Wash 2 cups of mung beans 2-3 times. Add washed mung beans to a deep bowl and add water until mung beans are covered completely. Keep overnight.
2. The next morning, throw away any water that is remaining in bowl. Wash the mung beans and transfer to a muslin cloth or cotton cloth and tie tightly. Put in a container and cover loosely with a lid. Keep in warm place anywhere in the kitchen for 24 hours and add some weight on top of the container and cloth.
3. You should see the sprouts the next day. *Note: In summer, mung beans will sprout quickly and may not need to be kept overnight.*

For Mung Salad

1. In a pan, add cooking oil, let it get a little warm, and add mung bean sprouts, salt, garlic, ginger and peppers. Cover and cook for 3-5 minutes.
2. Add green onion and red onion. Cook for another 3-6 minutes or until they are just soft, but not mushy.
3. Once done, add lime juice. Enjoy!

Cilantro Cucumber Dip

Servings: 2 | Prep time: 15 mins

EOC
~2mg

INGREDIENTS

- 1 cup Greek yogurt
- 2 small mini cucumber (finely chopped)
- 1 Tbsp dried cranberries
- 1 Tbsp chopped cilantro
- 2 tsp sugar
- ⅛ tsp salt (or per taste)
- ⅛ tsp serrano pepper (optional)

DIRECTIONS

1. Take a bowl and add yogurt, cucumber, cranberries, sugar and salt. Mix.
2. Top it off with cilantro and a few extra cranberries.

Zesty Cabbage Side

Servings: 4 | Prep time: 15 mins | Cook time: 20-25 mins

INGREDIENTS

- 5 cups shredded green cabbage
- ¼ tsp green chili paste
- ¼ tsp ginger paste
- 1 tsp salt or as per taste
- 1 cup carrots, chopped
- 1 Tbsp cooking oil
- ½ tsp mustard seeds
- ¼ cup cilantro leaves chopped

  Optional: green peas

EOC
~9mg

DIRECTIONS

1. Bring a small pot of water to a boil and add chopped carrots.
2. Let them cook for 10 minutes, strain, then set aside.
3. In a pan, add oil and mustard seeds. Sauté for a minute at low-medium flame. Add carrots and sauté for 1-2 minutes.
4. Add chili, ginger and salt. Mix.
5. Add shredded cabbage and let it cook for 8-10 minutes until slightly tender. Mix in-between as required.
6. Garnish with chopped cilantro leaves.

Virginia Ladner, RD

fitandnourishedlife.com

Virginia is a Registered Dietitian, group exercise instructor, and author of the Fit and Nourished Life blog. She is also a military spouse and mother of two, who currently lives in Israel.

Virginia graduated from the University of Alabama with both undergraduate and graduate degrees in nutrition. She has maintained registration as a dietitian through the Commission on Dietetic Registration (CDR) since January 2007. Her background consists of ample experience in both the hospital and outpatient settings.

Virginia's passion for instructing exercise classes started in college. She maintains certification as a group exercise instructor through the Athletics and Fitness Association of America (AFAA) and is licensed by the Zumba Instructor Network (ZIN). She teaches several types of fitness classes, both in person and virtually, including Zumba, sculpting, and high intensity interval training (HIIT).

Virginia's favorite role in life is caring for her 2 and 5 year-old children. Motherhood has provided Virginia with ample opportunities to refine her understanding and application of child nutrition. Additionally, she volunteers her dietitian knowledge and skills to support the local community. Most recently, she designed a nutrition program for the US Embassy in Israel's annual fitness challenge.

Eight years ago, doctors diagnosed Virginia with Type I diabetes. This discovery, along with caring for her family, has fueled Virginia's desire for finding the best ways to maintain a healthy lifestyle. Hoping to share this passion, Virginia started her Fit and Nourished Life blog, committed to life, food, nutrition, and fitness.

Chickpea Pancakes

Servings: 3 | Prep time: 5 mins | Cook time: 15 mins

EOC
~9mg

INGREDIENTS

- 1 ¼ cup chickpea flour
- 2 Tbsp granulated white sugar
- 1 Tbsp baking powder
- ½ tsp salt
- 2 Tbsp oil
- 1 cup milk
- 1 Tbsp butter

DIRECTIONS

1. Combine all dry ingredients.
2. Add liquid ingredients and stir until incorporated evenly but not smooth (should be lumpy).
3. Heat pan or griddle and add 1 Tbsp butter to pan.
4. Once butter is melted, spoon ¼ cup of batter onto hot pan or griddle. Cook until golden brown, flip and cook until brown again.

Cauliflower Shepherd's Pie

Servings: 4 | Prep time: 10-15 mins | Cook time: 30 mins

EOC
~9mg

INGREDIENTS

- 1 Tbsp olive oil or butter
- ½ medium onion, chopped
- 2 garlic cloves, minced
- 1 pound ground beef (round or loin)
- 2 Tbsp chickpea flour
- ½ cup milk
- 1 (15 ounce) can of peas (drained and rinsed for 20 seconds)
- 1 cup chicken broth
- 1 (10 ounce) package of frozen riced cauliflower
- 3 Tbsp cream cheese
- 2 Tbsp butter
- 1 egg, beaten until frothy
- Salt to taste

DIRECTIONS

1. Heat oven to 375°F.
2. Cook cauliflower according to package directions in a separate pot.
3. Heat oil/butter in large skillet. Add in garlic and onion. Cook until onion translucent and garlic is fragrant. Add in ground beef and cook until brown. Stir in flour and cook 1 minute. Add milk and cook until mixture starts to thicken slightly. Add in peas and broth and cook 5 more minutes, stirring frequently.
4. Drain cauliflower and return to pot. Add cream cheese, butter, and egg. Combine until blended well. Season with salt.
5. Spoon meat mixture into 8-inch square baking dish, cover with cauliflower mixture, then bake 15-20 minutes.

Seared Chicken with Multipurpose Green Sauce

Servings: 4
Prep time: 10-15 mins
Cook time: 10 mins

INGREDIENTS

For Green Sauce

- ½ cup sour cream
- ½ cup fresh cilantro
- ½ cup fresh dill
- 2 Tbsp olive oil
- 2 cloves garlic, minced
- Salt to taste

For Chicken

- 2 large boneless, skinless chicken breasts (cut in half horizontally)
- 1 Tbsp butter
- 2 Tbsp chickpea flour
- Salt to taste

INSTRUCTIONS

1. In a small food processor or blender, combine the sour cream, cilantro, dill, olive oil, and garlic. Process until smooth and creamy.
2. Add salt to taste.
3. If serving as a dressing, add a little water until at the desired consistency.
4. Place flour on a plate. Pat the chicken dry with a paper towel, and season chicken with salt on both sides.
5. Coat both sides of chicken with flour.
6. In a large pan, heat 1 Tbsp butter on medium-high heat until hot. Add the coated chicken and cook 3 to 5 minutes per side, or until golden brown and cooked through.

Sauce will stay fresh up to one week in the refrigerator.

EOC
~3mg

Salmon Cakes

Servings: 4 | Prep time: 5 mins | Cook time: 5-10 mins

INGREDIENTS

Salmon cakes

- 3 (3 oz) salmon fillets (skinned and chopped)
- ¼ cup chickpea flour
- ¼ cup mayonnaise
- 1 tsp lemon juice
- 1 egg yolk
- ½ tsp salt
- ½ tsp garlic powder
- 2 Tbsp olive oil (for cooking)

Dill Sauce

- ½ cup mayonnaise
- 1 clove garlic, minced
- ½ tsp lemon juice
- 1 tsp dried dill

EOC
~4mg

DIRECTIONS

1. Combine all ingredients, except olive oil (and dill sauce ingredients), and form into patties.
2. Add olive oil into heavy bottomed pan and heat until hot.
3. Cook patties for 2-3 minutes per side.
4. Combine all ingredients for dill sauce in a small bowl. Serve on top of salmon cakes.

Egg Muffins

Yield: 12 Muffins

Servings: 6
Prep time: 10 mins
Cook time: 30 mins

INGREDIENTS

- 1-2 Tbsp olive oil
- 1 small white onion, chopped
- 2 cloves garlic, minced
- 6 large eggs
- 3 Tbsp milk
- ¼ tsp paprika
- ½ tsp salt
- ½ cup shredded mozzarella cheese

DIRECTIONS

1. Heat oven to 350°F and grease a 12-cup muffin tin with cooking spray or olive oil.
2. In a large nonstick skillet over medium heat, cook onion and garlic until onion translucent and garlic fragrant.
3. In a small bowl, whisk eggs, milk, paprika and salt. Fold in cooked vegetable mixture and cheese. Pour mixture into prepared muffin tin.
4. Bake until cooked through and golden, approximately 30 minutes.
5. Let cool, then store in the fridge in an airtight container until ready to eat.

EOC
~2mg

Zahra Alipoursohi

IG: @zara.sohi | zarasohi.com

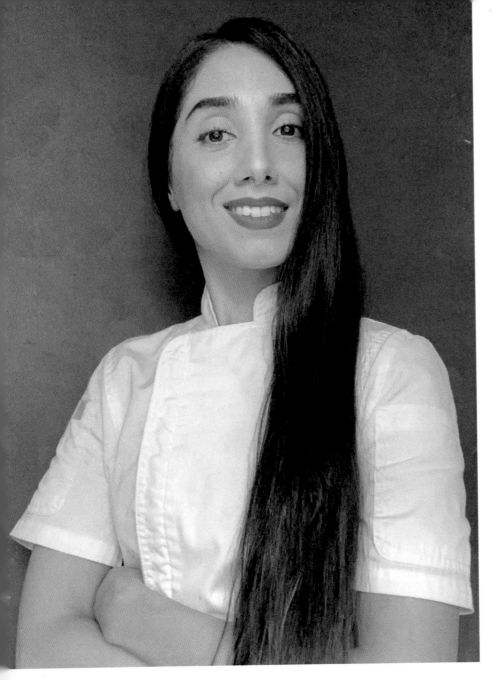

I was born and grew up in Tehran, Iran and now live in Danville, California. After I got my Bachelor's Degree in Pure Mathematics, I decided to go to culinary school and follow my childhood passion in food and pastry.

After almost three years, I got fourteen international certifications in baking and cooking from one of the best culinary schools in my country and a few more with other famous chefs.

To me, the kitchen is the heart and soul of a home. It is the place where people feel warm and comfortable, where the lovely aromas of soups, freshly baked bread, flaky pie crusts and fresh cakes permeate the rest of the house. As a kid, I remember flipping through my mom's vintage baking and cooking books, helping her to cook and attempting to recreate the recipes. I am lucky and thankful to have my dad, a chef, and my mom, both of whom taught me how to cook from a very young age.

I believe making food is not just about mixing ingredients, cooking, and eating. It is about adding your love as your magic to the ingredients and making that food fantastic. If I am being honest, I am obsessed with anything related to food and pastries, like the smells of herbs, the greatness, beauty and freshness of ingredients, and the aromas of different spices.

Cooking is like a form of meditation for me. I enjoy every step of it. It gives me a kind of power, knowing how to distinguish which herb or spice, fresh or dried, which combination of ingredients, or what kind of vegetables will give you the best and tastiest result. Also, I love to help people create new recipes with simple ingredients, and my goal is to inspire creativity in people who like cooking or baking, to help them cook with confidence like a real chef!

Buttery Shrimp on Endive Spears

Servings: 4
Prep time: 5 mins
Cook time: 5 mins

INGREDIENTS

- 1 pound shrimp
- 2 ½ Tbsp butter
- ½ tsp salt
- ¼ tsp red pepper
- 2 Tbsp lemon juice
- 1 medium avocado
- 2 Tbsp garlic, chopped
- 2 Tbsp fresh dill
- 4 medium-size endive leaves, pulled apart

INSTRUCTIONS

1. Place the butter in a medium pan and melt over medium-high heat.
2. Add the shrimp and season with salt, red pepper, and garlic.
3. Sauté for 3-4 minutes over medium heat, stirring occasionally, until shrimp are pink and cooked through.
4. Remove from heat and drizzle freshly squeezed lemon juice over the shrimp.
5. Mix the shrimp with sliced avocado and dill and serve spooned onto endive leaves. Garnish them with any fried garlic left in the pan.

EOC
~4mg

Baked Whole Trout with Dill Rice

Servings: 1 | Prep time: 15 mins + 30 mins for marinating | Cook time: 30 mins

INGREDIENTS

Trout

- 1 cleaned trout fish, or 2 filets
- ½ tsp salt
- 2 cloves garlic, minced
- 1 tsp melted butter
- 2 Tbsp chopped parsley
- 3 Tbsp olive oil
- 3 Tbsp lemon juice

Dill rice

- 1 cup rice
- ¼ tsp salt
- ⅓ cup finely chopped fresh dill
- 1 Tbsp butter
- ½ tsp liquid saffron
- 2 Tbsp olive oil

DIRECTIONS

1. In a bowl, marinate the inside of the fish, or the filets, with a mix of salt, garlic, 1 tsp melted butter, and half of the chopped parsley. Wrap and leave it to rest in the fridge for 30 minutes.
2. Rinse the rice in a medium sized bowl three times until water runs clean.
3. Boil 3 cups of water and add salt. Add the rice and let it cook for 4-5 minutes at medium-high heat, stirring throughout. Add the fresh dill to the rice in the last 10 seconds of cooking.
4. Use a colander to rinse off the rice and dill mixture.
5. Put 2 Tbsp olive oil in a small pot, then add liquid saffron and stir to combine.
6. Add rice and dill mixture to the pot and pour 1 Tbsp melted butter over the rice.
7. Cover and cook on low heat for about 20 minutes - until steam builds up.
8. While rice is cooking, add 3 Tbsp olive oil in a pan over medium-high heat, then add the trout. Cook it for about 5 minutes for each side until golden. If you use filets, they will only need about 3 minutes per side.
9. If you would like to serve the rice like a cake, place a dish over the pot and flip.
10. Add the lemon juice for serving and garnish with red pepper, parsley, and fried garlic.

Radish Salad

Servings: 2
Prep time: 30 mins

INGREDIENTS

- 3 cups thinly sliced radish
- 1 small, thinly sliced shallot
- 2 Tbsp chopped dill
- 1 Tbsp chopped parsley
- ½ Tbsp chopped cilantro
- 2 Tbsp lemon juice
- 1 tsp salt
- ½ tsp red pepper
- 2 medium cucumber
- 1 Tbsp chives
- 2 Tbsp olive oil
- 4 Tbsp Greek yogurt
- 2-3 Tbsp pumpkin seed

INSTRUCTIONS

1. Put the Greek yogurt, dill, parsley, cilantro, lemon juice, olive oil, chives, salt, and red pepper in a small bowl and whisk them. Cover and refrigerate the dressing bowl for at least 15 minutes before serving.
2. Thinly slice the radish, onion, cucumbers. You can also slice the radishes and onion up to two hours in advance, keep them in separate bowls, wrap and refrigerate them. I recommend against slicing the cucumber ahead of time because it will start to release water.
3. In a bowl, toss the radishes, onion, cucumbers, yogurt sauce, and pumpkin seeds. Mix well. Garnish the salad with fresh dill and radish slices.

EOC
~7mg

Creamy Red Lentil & Broccoli Soup

Servings: 3 | Prep time: 10 min | Cook time: 35 min

INGREDIENTS

- 1½ cups dry red lentil
- ½ large head broccoli
- ½ medium head cauliflower
- 1 medium onion
- 3 cloves, finely minced garlic
- 1 Tbsp oil
- ½ tsp salt
- ½ tsp white pepper
- 3 cups water
- 1 cup milk

INSTRUCTIONS

1. Add the olive oil, chopped onion, and minced garlic to a pot and sauté until the onions and garlic are softened.
2. Add the red lentil, broccoli, cauliflower, salt, pepper, and water and bring to a boil. Cover your pot with a lid, then reduce the heat to low, and simmer for 20-25 minutes. Soup is done when lentils are tender.
3. When your soup is cooked, use an immersion blender to blend it and make a purée. You can use the food processor if you do not have an immersion blender, just let it cool for 4-5 minutes before blending.
4. Once you are done blending, return it to the pot, and add the milk. Let it boil for 3-4 minutes over medium heat.
5. Top individual bowls of soup using chopped chives and cauliflower pieces for extra aesthetic.

This soup tastes amazing once it is properly salted. You can also add some lemon juice to make it tastier!

EOC
~17mg

Skirt Steak with Mashed Cauliflower & Roasted Garlic

Servings: 4 | Prep time: 20 mins, plus 4-5 hours to marinate | Cook time: 40 mins

INGREDIENTS

Skirt Steak

- 1 pound skirt steak, leaned of all exterior fat and connective tissue
- 2 Tbsp + ½ cup hot water
- 1 tsp saffron powder
- 4-5 cloves garlic, chopped
- 1 tsp grated fresh ginger
- 2 tsp soy sauce
- 1 tsp salt
- ½ tsp red pepper
- 3 Tbsp olive oil
- 1 cup fresh tamarind

Roasted Garlic

- 3-4 heads of garlic
- 3-4 tsp butter

EOC
~10mg

Mashed Cauliflower

- 1 medium head cauliflower, cut into florets
- 1 Tbsp butter
- 4 cloves garlic, minced
- 1 tsp salt
- ¼ tsp white pepper
- ¼ cup milk

DIRECTIONS

Skirt steak

1. In a medium bowl, add 1 tsp of the saffron powder to 2 Tbsp of the hot water. Let it rest for a few minutes.
2. Add the garlic, ginger, soy sauce, salt, red pepper and olive oil to the saffron powder mixture and whisk them together.
3. Pour the marinade over the steak, wrap the bowl, and put it in the fridge. Allow to marinate for 4-5 hours.
4. Add tamarind fruit to ½ cup hot water and let the mixture rest for 30 minutes. Discard tamarind fruit and add the liquid from the mixture to the steak/marinade combination for the last hour of marination.
5. Grill the steak over medium-high heat for 4 to 5 minutes per side, or to desired temperature, to serve it.

Roasted Garlic

1. Preheat the oven to 350°F.
2. Peel some outer layers of each whole garlic bulb. Use a sharp knife and cut a little bit off the top of the bulbs.
3. Put each one in a piece of aluminum foil, then add one tsp of butter on top of the garlic and cover with foil.
4. Place them on an oven pan and bake for 30-40 minutes until the cloves are lightly browned and feel soft when pressed.

Mashed Cauliflower

1. Add the cauliflower to a large pot of boiling water. Boil for about 10 minutes until soft and tender.
2. Drain and transfer to the food processor to make it a puree.
3. In a pot, heat the butter over medium-high heat. Sauté garlic for about 1 minute. Then add the cauliflower puree, milk, salt, and pepper to the pot and stir for 2-3 minutes. Garnish it with fried garlic.

Made in the USA
Middletown, DE
11 November 2022

14708534R00080